The International Dictionary of
GRAPHIC SYMBOLS

The International Dictionary of
GRAPHIC SYMBOLS

Joel Arnstein

Kogan Page

Editorial and Design:
John Simpson, Janet Scharf,
Barry Walsh

Illustration:
Mike Wortley, Joel Arnstein

Production:
Debra Adams, Julie Marston,
Sherrill Davies, Julia Talbut

First published in 1983 by Kogan Page Ltd,
120 Pentonville Road, London N1 9JN

British Library Cataloguing in Publication Data

Arnstein, Joel
   International dictionary of graphic symbols.
   1. Commercial art—Dictionaries
   2. Signs and symbols—Dictionaries
   I. Title
   741.6'0148   NC1280

   ISBN 0 85038 578 4

Printed in Great Britain in 1983 by
Whitstable Litho Ltd,
Whitstable, Kent

CONTENTS

This volume is a handbook for the identification and understanding of graphic symbols and is intended for both specialist and lay people in the subjects with which it deals. It includes symbols in domestic and everyday use, such as those on fabric care labels and road signs, and symbols used in technical spheres, such as architecture and electronics.

The symbols in this book are grouped together by subject and the various subjects listed alphabetically so as to provide a ready means of finding symbols when working within any particular field. Within each field, symbols are divided into sub-sections as appropriate to the subject. For initial reference purposes details of the sub-sections are given in the list of contents.

While this handbook covers the widest possible range of subjects, pottery and silver marks have had to be excluded as they are too numerous to detail satisfactorily in a book of this nature; for a similar reason, no attempt has been made to list all current trade marks and logos.

The symbols and explanations listed are believed to be those most widely accepted within the limitations described in the introduction to each section. Priority has been given to the inclusion of the symbols conforming to international practice. Symbols used primarily in the USA and the UK are included in areas where the use of international symbols has not been established. Certain nationally-used symbols which are commonly employed as alternatives to international symbols have also been given. Abbreviations and other additional information thought useful to the symbol reader are also included.

Today everyone encounters and needs to comprehend graphic symbols in a bewildering variety of forms and situations. That this should be the case thousands of years after the invention of the first alphabet may seem strange. However, today there is a great need for symbols that provide a quickly understandable means of communication without the language limitations of the written word in a world where technology is advancing rapidly and where trade, tourism, communications and legislation are becoming increasingly international. At the beginning of this century, Arabic numerals and musical notation were the only symbol systems with any of the attributes of a universal language. Today, more and more forms of symbol are achieving a similar status. This book, it is hoped, will provide some assistance in improving general understanding and communication.

ACKNOWLEDGEMENTS

Material from British Standards is reproduced by permission of the British Standards Institution, 2 Park Street, London W1A 2BS from whom complete copies of the standards can be obtained. I would like to thank the Institution and the other publishers who granted permission for their material to be republished:

ANSI Standards Z32.2.3 – 1949 (r 1953) and *Z32.2.4 – 1949 (r 1953)* – American National Standards Institute (these standards were originated by the American Society of Mechanical Engineers who kindly granted permission for material from them to be used in this book)

Architectural Graphic Standards (7th edn, 1981), Ramsey/Sleeper – John Wiley and Sons, Inc

British Admiralty Chart no 5011 – certain nautical chart symbols conforming to international practice were reproduced from this 'chart' (book of chart symbols) by permission of the Controller, HM Stationery Office, and the Hydrographer of the Navy

Cartographic Technical Standards – TS Paper 4.02.1 dated 11/11/77 (geological symbols) – US Geological Survey (US Department of the Interior)

Chart Specifications of the IHO (sections 300 and 400) – International Hydrographic Bureau

DIN/ISO Standard 4067 Part 1 – Deutsches Institut für Normung e. V.

European rules concerning road traffic, signs and signals (Feb 1974) – European Conference of Ministers of Transport (produced by OECD Publications, Paris)

Heraldry: Customs, Rules and Styles, Carl Alexander von Volborth – Blandford Press

Heraldry of the World, Carl Alexander von Volborth – Blandford Press

International Legend for Hydrogeological Maps (1970) – UNESCO

Norton's Star Atlas (17th edn, 1978) – Gall and Inglis Ltd

SI, The International System of Units (1977) – the National Physical Laboratory (translated from 'Le Systeme International d'Unites' published by BIPM)

Standard Geological Symbols (legend produced by Department of National Development, Canberra) as published in *Field Geologists Manual*, Berkman (1976) – the Australian Institute of Mining and Metallurgy

Standard Highway Signs (1979) – US Department of Transportation

Standard Legend (1976) – Shell Internationale Petroleum Maatschappij BV, the Hague

Standard Method of Detailing Reinforced Concrete – The Concrete Society

(The) Traffic Signs Regulations and General Directions 1981, Statutory Instrument No. 859 – HM Stationery Office (British traffic signs are reproduced in this book by permission of the Controller, HM Stationery Office)

United States Road Symbol Signs (1979) – US Department of Transportation

Units of Measurement – ISO Standards Handbook 2 (2nd edn, 1982) – International Organisation for Standardization

Topographic map symbols are reproduced with permission of the Ordnance Survey and the US Geological Survey (US Department of the Interior)

I am grateful for the advice and assistance towards the production of this book that I have received from so many people and organisations. I would like especially to thank the following:

Hugh Atkinson BA (Hons)
S J Bridger MCIBS
Andrew Conway BSc, AIA
Bridget Crouch
Dick Marshall
Robert Smith C Eng, FI Struct E, M Cons E
K C Sugden PhD, FRAS
Gene M Wilhoite, PE Consultant
John Wilson BSc (Hons)
Thomas Woodcock, Somerset Herald
The American Institute of Architects
The American Institute of Steel Construction
The American Society of Civil Engineers
Bund Deutscher Architekten
The Concrete Society
GINETEX (the International Association for Textile Care Labelling)
Lehigh Structural Steel Co
The Royal Architectural Institute of Canada

In addition to the above people, I would also like to thank for their assistance the librarians at the Institute of Geological Sciences, the Institution of Structural Engineers, the London School of Economics, the Royal Astronomical Society and the Royal Institute of British Architects, and the staff of Kogan Page.

Architectural drawings are used to explain proposed projects to lay people and to issue instructions to builders.

The graphic symbols and conventions in this section are used in such drawings and are widely understood by those people associated with the building industry. However, there is no universally accepted standard for architectural symbols. Drawing and style vary between countries, regions, architectural practices and between individual draughtsmen. As a result, such symbols should be considered to be merely aids towards drawing clarity, without the precision of meaning to be found, for instance, in musical or mathematical notation. Written specification is often required to define the meaning further.

For other symbols frequently incorporated into production drawings, see *Electrical, Engineering (Civil and Structural)* and *Engineering (Plumbing, Ventilation and Ductwork)*.

LINES

Note: Lines are normally thicker where the construction shown is 'cut through' or in section.

hidden detail or **existing construction to be removed** — — — — —

break line used in delineating partially drawn objects, except for partially drawn cylindrical objects

alternative to above symbol

alternative to above symbol

break in solid cylinder, eg rod, rail, column

break in hollow cylinder, eg pipe

centre line or **axis** or **structural grid line** or **section line**

repeated features

can be indicated by one drawn object and the centre lines of the remainder, as above

property/boundary line — - - — - - —

ARROW FORMS AND ALTERNATIVES

Note: All the arrow forms and graphic alternatives in this section are in common use. However, it is desirable that, within any one body of drawings, a limited selection of arrow forms (with set functions and a recognizable hierarchy) is adopted.

open arrow

solid arrows

ARCHITECTURE

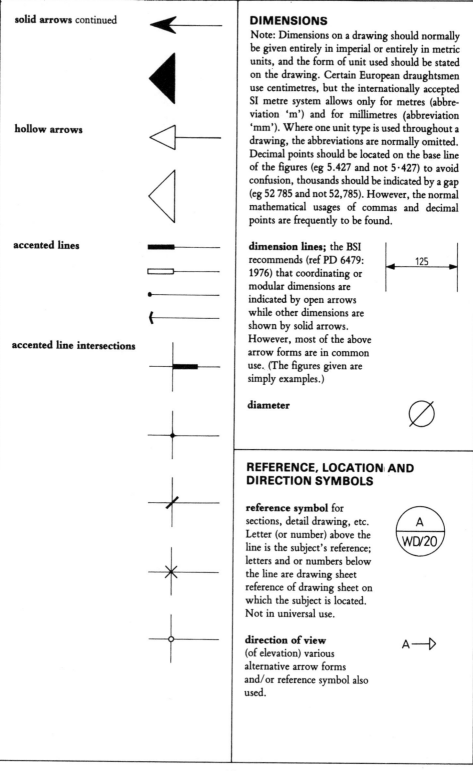

solid arrows continued

hollow arrows

accented lines

accented line intersections

DIMENSIONS

Note: Dimensions on a drawing should normally be given entirely in imperial or entirely in metric units, and the form of unit used should be stated on the drawing. Certain European draughtsmen use centimetres, but the internationally accepted SI metre system allows only for metres (abbreviation 'm') and for millimetres (abbreviation 'mm'). Where one unit type is used throughout a drawing, the abbreviations are normally omitted. Decimal points should be located on the base line of the figures (eg 5.427 and not 5·427) to avoid confusion, thousands should be indicated by a gap (eg 52 785 and not 52,785). However, the normal mathematical usages of commas and decimal points are frequently to be found.

dimension lines; the BSI recommends (ref PD 6479: 1976) that coordinating or modular dimensions are indicated by open arrows while other dimensions are shown by solid arrows. However, most of the above arrow forms are in common use. (The figures given are simply examples.)

125

diameter

REFERENCE, LOCATION AND DIRECTION SYMBOLS

reference symbol for sections, detail drawing, etc. Letter (or number) above the line is the subject's reference; letters and or numbers below the line are drawing sheet reference of drawing sheet on which the subject is located. Not in universal use.

A
WD/20

direction of view (of elevation) various alternative arrow forms and/or reference symbol also used.

A ➔

section line

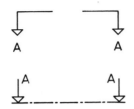

defines the location of the plane of the section or 'cut through', the arrow(s) indicate(s) the direction of view, adjacent letter(s) (and/or numbers) give(s) the section's reference. To avoid visual confusion, only a small part of the line may be drawn (forming a right-angled corner with the arrow shaft), or the line is drawn as a dot-dash line or a line of different thickness to other lines forming the drawing.

Alternative arrow forms and/or reference symbols are also used; eg

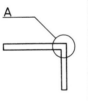

detail reference giving location of detail. The circle, indicating the area enlarged in the detail drawing, may be omitted and the general area of the detail indicated by one of the arrow forms. The reference symbol may also be incorporated.

north symbol, drawn on to plans to give the orientation of building. Alternative arrow forms may be used within the circle to form this symbol. The letter 'N' may be incorporated. Sometimes a secondary arrow indicating magnetic north is added.

alternative to above symbol

MATERIALS — shown in section

Note: The symbolic 'textures' are normally used, filling only the extremities of the drawing. Those marked 'BS 1192' are in accordance with British Standard.

General

all **materials in section**

all **hidden or adjacent parts** in section

Ground

earth/compact fill

made ground/refill, alternative to above symbol (or blockwork)

gravel/porous fill

hardcore

rock

sand (or screed; mortar; plaster; cut stone)

ARCHITECTURE

Concrete

concrete, general symbol (BS 1192), lightweight concrete

in situ/precast concrete

alternative to above symbol (or copper alloy; stone)

concrete (may be lightly shaded), alternative to the above concrete symbols

screed (BS 1192) (or mortar; plaster; cut stone; sand)

concrete blockwork (small-scale)

concrete blockwork (large scale) (or made ground)

Brick

brick (BS 1192)

common-face brick (or metal)

fire brick

structural facing tile

Stone

stone (BS 1192) (or copper alloy)

alternative to above symbol

cut stone (or screed; mortar; plaster; sand)

bluestone/slate/soapstone flagging

rubble

marble

Adobe rammed earth

alternative (a)

alternative (b)

Timber

unwrot (BS 1192)

wrot (BS 1192)

blocking

plywood (small-scale)

plywood (large-scale)

blockboard

alternative to above symbol

Metal

metal general symbol (small-scale)

metal general symbol (large-scale) (or common-face brick)

copper alloy brass, bronze, gunmetal, etc (large-scale) (or in situ/precast concrete; stone)

examples of alternative patterns used to distinguish between various ferrous and non-ferrous metals (large-scale)

alternative (a)

alternative (b)

alternative (c)

Glass

glass

structural glass

glass brick or block

Plastic

plastic

Plaster

plaster (or screed; mortar; cut stone; sand)

metal lath and plaster

gypsum wallboard/plasterboard

Insulation

insulation, general symbol/glass or mineral fibre quilt/batt/loose fill

sprayed/foamed

alternative to above symbol

rigid

alternative to above symbol

Finishes

acoustic tile

ceramic tile (small-scale)

ceramic tile (large-scale)

terrazzo

plastic laminate

PVC/linoleum/rubber

MATERIALS — shown in elevation

plaster/concrete

ARCHITECTURE

brick

shingles

glass

ceramic tile

sheet metal

**MOVABLE BUILDING ELEMENTS —
doors, windows, hatches, etc (in
elevation)**

Hinged
Note: The hinged side is indicated by dotted lines
radiating from the centre of the hinged side to the
far opposite corners of the element. It is to be
assumed that, unless specified otherwise, side and
top hinged windows open out and bottom hinged
windows open in.

hinged on left-hand side

alternative to above symbol

hinged at top

alternative to above symbol

Pivoted
Note: Location of pivots indicated by short
lines.

vertically pivoted

alternative to above symbol

horizontally pivoted

alternative to above symbol

Sliding
Note: Direction of opening is shown by arrow.

vertically sliding
(sash window)

horizontally sliding
(patio door with fixed
element)

Note: The above is sometimes shown by fine
straight lines, not arcs.

single swing door

double door, double swing

alternative to above symbol

BUILDING ELEMENTS — in plan view

Stairs and Ramps
The arrow should give direction of rise. Treads
should be numbered from the lowest point.

stair

1 2 3 4 5 6

ramp

1:8

Doors (or similar hinged element)
direction of opening or movement of each leaf
should be shown by an arc.

single swing door

double door, double swing

alternative to above symbol

Partitions
See also *Materials* above for brickwork,
blockwork, etc

timber studwork

alternative to above
symbol

metal studwork

alternative to above
symbol

**window/glazed
opening in wall**

alternative to above
symbol

alternative to above
symbol

ASTROLOGY

The symbols given in this section are used in Western astrology.

The principal astrological signs are known as the 'Signs of the Zodiac' or 'Sun Signs'. The zodiac is an imaginary band around the sky, 18 degrees wide, and with the ecliptic (the apparent annual, not daily, path of the sun) along its centre. The zodiac is divided into 12 equal sections; in each of which a particular group of fixed stars or a constellation can be seen. As the year progresses, the sun appears to be located for one month in each constellation in turn. These constellations are the Signs of the Zodiac – the symbols for which are given in this section. The sign the Sun is 'in' at the time of a person's birth is their 'Sun-sign' or 'birth-sign' and is considered of particular significance.

The apparent movements of the Moon and planets are confined within the band of the zodiac, and are also of great significance in astrology. See *Astronomy* for symbols for the Moon and planets.

A horoscope is normally drawn in the form of a circular chart, representing the zodiac, and shows the locations of the stars, Sun, Moon and planets relative to each other and to the subject at a particular time, date and place (usually the time, date and place of the subject's birth).

An aspect is the angle formed between two celestial bodies, or points, and the earth. It is believed that the aspects arising from the relative locations of celestial bodies affect their various influences. Conjunction, sextile, square, trine and opposition are generally considered to be the major aspects.

SIGNS OF THE ZODIAC
Note: The symbols below may be drawn with minor variations.

Aquarius the Water-Carrier
(21 January to 19 February)

alternative to above symbol

Pisces the Fish
(20 February to 20 March)

Aries the Ram
(21 March to 20 April), or the
First Point in Aries
(see *Astronomy*)

Taurus the Bull
(21 April to 21 May)

Gemini the Twins
(22 May to 21 June)

alternative to above symbol

Cancer the Crab
(22 June to 22 July)

alternative to above symbol

Leo the Lion
(23 July to 23 August)

alternative to above symbol	♌
Virgo the Virgin (23 August to 23 September)	♍
alternative to above symbol	♍
Libra the Scales (24 September to 23 October), or the First Point in Libra (see *Astronomy*)	♎
Scorpio the Scorpion (24 October to 22 November)	♏
alternative to above symbol	♏
Sagittarius the Archer (23 November to 21 December)	♐
alternative to above symbol	♐
Capricorn the Goat (22 December to 20 January)	♑
alternative to above symbol	♑

conjunction (0°, a direct, or almost direct, line-up of celestial points viewed from the earth)	☌
semi-sextile (30°)	⊻
semi-square (45°)	∠
sextile (60°)	✳
square (90°)	□
trine (120°)	△
sesqui-quadrate (135°)	⟤
quincunx (150°)	⟑
opposition (180°)	☍
alternative to above symbol	⚮
ascending node (north node), the point where a celestial body crosses the ecliptic from south to north	☊
descending node (south node), the point where a celestial body crosses the ecliptic from north to south	☋

Note: In astrology, the nodes of the moon are generally considered of greatest significance. In astronomy, the nodes may refer to the point of intersection of any reference plane (including the plane of the ecliptic) and the orbit of a celestial body.

ASPECTS

Note: An aspect is normally still considerd to exist even if the relative locations of celestial points deviate within certain limits from the ideal angles given below as each aspect is considered to have an 'orb of influence'.

ASTRONOMY

In addition to the symbols given below, the 'Signs of the Zodiac' may be used to denote zodiacal constellations. The signs for aspects and for ascending and descending nodes may be used to indicate the relative physical locations of celestial bodies. These symbols are given under *Astrology*.

Stellar nomenclature
Apart from a few exceptions, traditional star names are rarely used today. Instead the nomenclature of bright stars is generally in accordance with a system devised by Bayer in 1603, whereby a bright star is denoted by a Greek letter followed by the Latin name (in the genitive case) of the constellation; eg the star Altair in the constellation Aquila may be referred to as α Aquilae. Usually the brightest star in each constellation is denoted α, the second brightest β and so on; although, in certain constellations, the Greek letter simply denotes a star's location. In Bayer's system, after the Greek alphabet was exhausted in any constellation, the lower case Roman letters, a,b,c, etc, were employed; followed by the Roman capital letters from A to Q. Under a system devised by Argelander, variable stars are denoted by the capital letters R,S,T, etc to Z or the double form AA to AZ, BA to BZ, etc to ZZ (omitting J) — eg HR Delphini. Alternatively variable stars may be denoted by the abbreviation V, v or VAR, and a number.

Any fainter star, to which no letter has been assigned, is referred to by its number in Flamstead's *Historia Caelestis Britannica* (published 1725), followed by the genitive case of the constellation in which it is located. If no Flamstead number exists for a particular star, the reference number from some other star catalogue is used and the catalogue referred to by name or an abbreviation of its name (no reference to a constellation being made in this case). Normally star catalogues also number stars assigned with Greek letters and/or Flamstead numbers.

The brighter nebulae and star clusters are generally referred to by their numbers in Messier's catalogue of 103 nebulae and clusters (published 1784) or in the *New General Catalogue* of Sir John Herschel (published 1888) — prefixed by the abbreviation M or NGC respectively.

Celestial sphere
The relative positions of stars and other celestial bodies are most frequently described and mapped in relation to the celestial sphere. The celestial sphere is an imaginary immense sphere with (usually) Earth at its centre and its radius extending beyond any celestial body being considered so that each celestial body can be mapped by being projected onto the inner surface of the sphere. The celestial sphere, in effect, represents the complete sky as seen by an observer. In general, as the celestial sphere is so immense, Earth's own radius can be ignored and the locations of objects on the sphere are the same whether viewed from Earth's centre or on its surface. The celestial sphere apears to rotate east to west every 23 hours 56 minutes as Earth rotates daily west to east (see *sideral time* below).

The coordinate system, commonly used in star charts or maps of the celestial sphere, has the celestial equator (Earth's equator projected onto the celestial sphere) as the fundamental great circle and celestial poles of north and south; ie the Earth's poles projected onto the celestial sphere. Alternative coordinate systems, used in regard to the celestial sphere, employ the ecliptic (the Sun's apparent annual path around the celestial sphere), or an observer's horizon (horizontal plane) projected onto the celestial sphere, or the galactic equator (the path of the galaxy traced on the celestial sphere) as fundamental great circles. The galactic equator lies on the galactic plane which is, as near as possible, the central plane through the spiral of the Galaxy.

Units of distance

The great distances considered in astronomy are expressed in terms of parsecs (see *Stellar Astronomy* below), light years and astronomical units. An astronomical unit (abbreviation AU) is 149,600,000 km; approximately the mean distance of the Sun from Earth. A light year (abbreviation ly) is the distance travelled in one year by a particle moving at the speed of light; ie 63,240 AU or 94,607 x 10^8 km.

THE PLANETS

Mercury

Venus

Earth

alternative to above symbol

Mars

Jupiter

Saturn

Uranus

alternative to above symbol

Neptune

alternative to above symbol

Pluto

alternative to above symbol

alternative to above symbol

ASTRONOMY

OTHER CELESTIAL BODIES
ie asteroid, Sun, Moon and star symbols

Ceres
(asteroid or minor planet)

Vesta
(asteroid or minor planet)

Pallas
(asteroid or minor planet)

Juno
(asteroid or minor planet)

Sun; may be used in
statements of comparison, eg
'mass 250⊙' (meaning a mass
of 250 times that of the sun)

Moon

alternative to above symbol

new Moon

first quarter

alternative to above symbol

full Moon

last quarter

alternative to above symbol

eclipse of the Moon

star

alternative to above symbol

SPHERICAL AND POSITIONAL ASTRONOMY

First Point in Aries (vernal
equinox), the zero point for both
the equatorial and the ecliptic
coordinate systems — one of the
two points where the ecliptic
intersects the celestial equator (the
sun crosses the celestial equator
from south to north at this point).
Because of precession of the earth's
axis, the First Point of Aries now
lies in Pisces. — Υ

First Point in Libra (autumnal
equinox), one of the two points
where the ecliptic intersects the
celestial equator and the point
where the sun crosses the celestial
equator from north to south.
Because of precession of the earth's
axis, this point now lies in Virgo. — $\simeq$

azimuth, the angle between an
observer's meridian plane and the
vertical plane through a celestial
object — A

alternative to above symbol — Az

altitude, a celestial object's vertical
angular distance above (north) or
below (south) of the horizon — h

zenith distance, the zenith is the point directly above an observer — Z

altitude of north pole — ϕ

alternative to above symbol — φ

hour angle (normally expressed in hours, minutes and seconds), the angle along the celestial equator between the hour circle of an object and an observer's meridian — H

alternative to above symbol — t

declination, the angular distance of an object north or south of the celestial equator — δ

right ascension, the angle along the celestial equator between the hour circle through an object and the First Point in Aries — α

sideral time, 'star time', measured by the apparent daily rotation of the fixed stars around the earth. — θ

Note: A sideral (stellar) day = 23 hours 56 minutes, 4 minutes shorter than the solar day as the Sun moves daily through 4 minutes of right ascension of the celestial sphere.

sideral time at mean midnight — θ_o

equation of time, true solar time minus mean solar time, ie apparent solar time minus accurate 'clock' time — E

geographical longitude, angular distance from a standard meridian — positive towards west, negative towards east — L

geographical latitude, positive north of the equator, negative south of the equator — ϕ

alternative to the above symbol — φ

obliquity of the ecliptic, the angle the ecliptic is inclined to the celestial equator (about 23° 27′) — $\in$

geocentric longitude — λ

geocentric latitude — β

heliocentric longitude — l

heliocentric latitude — b

Note: A heliocentric celestial sphere has the centre of the Sun as its centre.

acceleration due to gravity — g

equatorial horizontal parallax, the angle between the direction to the earth's centre and the direction to an observer on the equator from a celestial object on the horizon, ie the maximum geocentric parallax — $P_?$

general precession in longitude in one tropical year — p

lunar-solar precession in one tropical year — p_1

planetary precession in one tropical year — p_2

annual precession in right ascension — P_a

annual precession in declination — p_δ

Note: In astronomy, 'precession' normally refers to the gradual alteration in the direction of the polar axis of the Earth (due to the gravitational effect of other bodies — in particular, the Sun and the Moon) or the resultant change in the co-ordinates of the celestial sphere relative to the Earth.

observed clock **time of transit** — T

Note: A 'transit' normally means either the passage of Mars or Venus across the Sun's disc or the passage of a star across an observer's celestial meridian, but also may refer to the passing of a planetary satellite or its shadow across the face of a planet.

clock correction (positive if clock is slow) — ΔT

ASTRONOMY

angular distance, the observed angle between two celestial objects (normally given in degrees, minutes and seconds) — d

CELESTIAL MECHANICS

semi-major axis, the maximum distance from the centre of an ellipse (or elliptical orbit) to its edge — a

eccentricity, the extent an elliptical orbit deviates from circularity (for a circular orbit $e = 0$, for the Earth's orbit $e = 0.016722$) — e

inclination, the angle between the plane of a celestial object's orbit and the plane of the ecliptic — i

longitude of ascending node, the angular distance from the First Point in Aries to the ascending node (the point where an object passes through a reference plane — usually the plane of the ecliptic) — Ω

longitude of perihelion (the perihelion is the point nearest the Sun in the orbit of any solar-orbiting body) — w

perihelion time — T

perihelion distance — q

time of epoch or reference moment in time — T

mean angular motion per solar day — n

gravitational constant — G

Caussian gravitational constant (0.017207098950 radian or 3548.187607 arc seconds) — k

planetary mass in units of solar mass — m

time of observation — t

angle of eccentricity, defined by $e = \sin$ — ϕ

alternative to above symbol — φ

orbital period — P

true anomaly, the angle at the focus of an elliptical orbit between the orbiting object and the point of nearest approach to the focus (the periapsis) of the orbit — ν

mean anomaly, the angle that would exist at the focus of an elliptical orbit between the orbiting object and the point of nearest approach to the focus (the periapsis) of the orbit, if in constant motion — M

mean anomaly at epoch — M_0

eccentric anomaly, the angle, at the centre of an elliptical orbit, between the periapsis (point of nearest approach to the focus) and the position of the orbiting object projected by a line perpendicular to the orbit's major axis — E

radius vector from the center of the Sun — r

distance between the centres of the Sun and Earth — R

the Sun's geocentric longitude with reference to the ecliptic — $\odot$

alternative to above symbol — L

geocentric distance of an object — Δ

STELLAR ASTRONOMY

ånström unit, unit used in the measurement of wavelengths (named after the spectroscopist AJ Ångström), one Å = one ten-millionth of a millimetre; visible light has a wavelength of between 3,900 Å and 15,000 Å — $Å$

intensity, the energy radiated per unit solid angle from a point source I

luminosity, the total energy radiated per second from a star, ie its absolute brightness $\mathscr{L}$

apparent magnitude, the brightness of a celestial object as apparent from Earth m

apparent visual magnitude m_v

apparent photographic magnitude m_{pg}

apparent photovisual magnitude m_{pv}

apparent radiometric magnitude m_{rad}

apparent bolometric magnitude m_{bol}

Note: The above are forms of magnitude determined by different methods giving different results. Apparent bolometric magnitude is an indicator of the total of all forms of radiation reaching Earth from a celestial body, ie that recorded by a bolometer.

absolute magnitude, magnitude of a celestial body at the standard distance of 10 parsecs (indices as for m) M

colour excess, an excess of the measured value of the colour index of a star over the expected value; an indicator of the reddening of a star as a result of intervening stellar dust E

wavelength λ

effective wavelength λ_e

effective temperature, the surface temperature of a star found by calculating the surface temperature of a perfect radiator (a black body) of the same radius as the star and emitting the same total energy. (Always less than the equivalent colour temperature.) T_e

colour temperature, the surface temperature of a star found by matching the distribution of energy in the continuous spectrum emitted by the star to that which would be emitted by a perfect radiator (a black body) of calculable temperature T_c

radial velocity, the speed of a celestial object towards or away from an observer V

tangential velocity, the speed of angular movement of a celestial object relative to the celestial sphere, ie across the line of sight of an observer T

spatial velocity W

distance in parsecs, a parsec is the distance at which one astronomical unit subtends an angle of one arc second, ie 206,265 AU or 3.2616 ly r

abbreviation for **parsec,** alternative to above symbol pc

galactic longitude, the angular distance eastwards along the galactic equator from the presumed galactic centre (0°) in the constellation Sagittarius l

galactic latitude, the angular distance north (positive) or south (negative) of the galactic equator b

Note: 1′ and b′ are the galactic coordinates in accordance with the pre-1959 system; while 1″ and b″ denote the coordinates of the system adopted by the International Astronomical Union in 1959.

total proper motion in seconds of arc per year μ

proper motion in right ascension in seconds of time per year μ_α

ASTRONOMY

proper motion in right
declination in seconds of arc per
year μ_δ

Note: 'Proper motion' of a star is its apparent
angular movement relative to the celestial sphere,
ie across the line of vision.

absorbtion coefficient in
interstellar space expressed in
magnitudes per 1000 parsecs a

SIGNIFICANCE OF PLUS AND MINUS

direction
+ (a) northwards, (b) 'direct' or 'positive'
  motion — ie to the left or eastwards, when
  looking south
− (a) southwards, (b) 'retrograde' or
  'negative' motion — ie to the right, or
  westwards, when looking south

variable stars
+ the maximum or minimum is later than
  the predicted date
− the maximum or minimum is earlier than
  the predicted date

comets
+ later than ephemeris prediction
− earlier than ephemeris prediction

planetographic declination of the Earth
+ the planet's north pole is tilted towards the
  Earth
− the planet's south pole is tilted towards the
  Earth

declination
+ north of celestial equator
− south of celestial equator

latitude
+ north of equator
− south of equator

longitude
+ west of prime meridian
− east of prime meridian

libration (in latitude)
+ mean centre displaced to south
− mean centre displaced to north

libration (in longitude)
+ mean centre displaced to east
− mean centre displaced to west

light-time
+ later
− earlier

magnitude
+ fainter than mag 0·0
− brighter than mag 0·0

position angle of the Sun's axis
+ north pole east of the hour circle
− north pole west of the hour circle

proper motion and precession
(in declination)
+ northwards
− southwards

proper motion and precession
(in right ascension)
+ direct
− retrograde

radial velocity
+ receding from the Sun
− approaching the Sun

Saturn's Rings
+ Earth north of ring-plane
− Earth south of ring-plane

the Sun's equator
+ south of disk centre
− north of disk centre

IAU ABBREVIATIONS FOR THE CONSTELLATIONS

Note: The following are the constellations' Latin
names, nominative and genitive, and three-letter
abbreviations, published by the International
Astronomical Union in 1966, which are in general
use.

And Andromeda, Andromedae
Ant Antlia, Antliae
Aps Apus, Apodis
Aqr Aquarius, Aquarii
Aql Aquila, Aquilae
Ara Ara, Arae
Ari Aries, Arietis

Aur	Auriga, Aurigae		**Lip**	Libra, Librae
Boo	Bootes, Bootis		**Lup**	Lupus, Lupi
Cae	Caelum, Caeli		**Lyn**	Lynx, Lyncis
Cam	Camelopardalis, Camelopardalis		**Lyr**	Lyra, Lyrae
Cnc	Cancer, Cancri		**Men**	Mensa, Mensae
CVn	Canes Venatici, Canum Venaticorum		**Mic**	Microscopium, Microscopii
CMa	Canis Major, Canis Majoris		**Mon**	Monoceros, Monocerotis
CMi	Canis Minor, Canis Minoris		**Mus**	Musca, Muscae
Cap	Capricornus, Capricorni		**Nor**	Norma, Normae
Car	Carina, Carinae		**Oct**	Octans, Octantis
Cas	Cassiopeia, Cassiopeiae		**Oph**	Ophiuchus, Ophiuchi
Cen	Centaurus, Centauri		**Ori**	Orion, Orionis
Cep	Cepheus, Cephei		**Pav**	Pavo, Pavonis
Cet	Cetus, Ceti		**Peg**	Pegasus, Pegasi
Cha	Chamaeleon, Chamaeleontis		**Per**	Perseus, Persei
Cir	Circinus, Circini		**Phe**	Phoenix, Phoenicis
Col	Columba, Columbae		**Pic**	Pictor, Pictoris
Com	Coma Berenices, Comae Berenices		**Psc**	Pisces, Piscium
CrA	Corona Austrina, Coronae Austrinae		**PsA**	Piscis Austrinus, Piscis Austrini
CrB	Corono Borealis, Coronae Borealis		**Pup**	Puppis, Puppis
Crv	Corvus, Corvi		**Pyx**	Pyxis, Pyxidis
Crt	Crater, Crateris		**Ret**	Reticulum, Reticuli
Cru	Crux, Crucis		**Sge**	Sagitta, Sagittae
Cyg	Cygnus, Cygni		**Sgr**	Sagittarius, Sagittarii
Del	Delphinus, Delphini		**Sco**	Scorpius, Scorpii
Dor	Dorado, Doradus		**Scl**	Sculptor, Sculptoris
Dra	Draco, Draconis		**Sct**	Scutum, Scuti
Equ	Equuleus, Equulei		**Ser**	Serpens, Serpentis
Eri	Eridanus, Eridani		**Sex**	Sextans, Sextantis
For	Fornax, Fornacis		**Tau**	Tauris, Tauri
Gem	Gemini, Geminorum		**Tel**	Telescopium, Telescopii
Gru	Grus, Gruis		**Tri**	Triangulum, Trianguli
Her	Hercules, Herculis		**TrA**	Triangulum Australe, Trianguli Australis
Hor	Horologium, Horologii			
Hay	Hydra, Hydrae		**Tuc**	Tucana, Tucanae
Hyi	Hydrus, Hydri		**UMa**	Ursa Major, Ursae Majoris
Ind	Indus, Indi		**UMi**	Ursa Minor, Ursae Minoris
Lae	Lacerta, Lacertae		**Vel**	Vela, Velorum
Leo	Leo, Leonis		**Vir**	Virgo, Virginis
LMi	Leo Minor, Leonis Minoris		**Vol**	Volans, Volantis
Lep	Lepus, Leporis		**Vul**	Vulpecula, Vulpeculae

BIOLOGY

The symbols and abbreviations in this section may be found in books and documents on botany, zoology, gardening, farming, plant and animal breeding, and genetics.

For symbols and abbreviations for chemical elements and processes, see *Chemistry*.

Plant and animal *nomenclature* — the scientific or 'Latin' names of species, following a system devised by Carl Linnaeus — primarily consist of two parts: the name of the genus (written with an initial capital letter), followed by a word describing or specifying the species within the genus (with initial lower-case). If a name is repeated in any context, it is common practice for the generic name to be abbreviated to its initial letter. The name of the person who first so-named a species may be given as a third part to its name and is then often given in the form of an abbreviation. Thus Common Quaking-Grass may be referred to as Briza media L (the 'L' referring to Linnaeus who first classified the plant) and subsequently referred to as B media L or B media. Sub-species may be referred to by three-part names: the first indicating the genus; the second, the species, and the third, the sub-species.

BOTANICAL AND ZOOLOGICAL SYMBOLS

female ♀

male ♂

hermaphrodite or, in reference to plants, polygamous (ie bearing flowers with stamens (male flowers), flowers with pistils (female flowers) and flowers with both, on the same or on different plants ☿

alternative to above symbol ♂♀

hybrid, mated to, cross-fertilized with. Beside illustrations, the symbol may imply the degree of magnification, ie 'times' (eg X2 meaning the illustration is twice actual size) ✕

of the **first filial** generation (ie the direct offspring); if a plant or animal of one genetic strain is crossed with one of another, the offspring are F_1 hybrids (first generation crosses) F_1

of the **second filial** generation; an F_2 generation is the progeny arising from the self-fertilization of F_1 offspring or from fertilization between F_1 offspring F_2

R_2 progeny or members of an R_2 generation arise from a **back-cross** between an F_1 individual and one of its parents R_2

Note: *Dominant genetic characteristics* are normally denoted by capital letter abbreviations; while *recessive genetic characteristics* are normally denoted by lower-case letter abbreviations.

gamete chromosome number, ie the number of chromosomes in a gamete cell n

diploid chromosome number. ie the number of chromosomes in a diploid cell $2n$

personally verified, plant seen by the writer !

BOTANICAL ABBREVIATIONS

A	annual (lives for one year)
ann	alternative to above
B	biennial (normally lives or is grown for two years: in gardening, this normally implies the plant is sown and grown one year to flower or fruit the next)
fl	flower, flowering
fls	flowers
fr	fruit, fruiting
frs	fruits
HA	hardy annual (annual which generally may be sown out-doors without protection against cold, in spring)
HB	hardy biennial (biennial that may be grown without special protection against cold)
HHA	half-hardy annual (annual which generally requires artificial warmth or protection against cold when sown, and as a seedling, in spring)
HHP	half-hardy perennial (normally a perennial requiring artificial warmth or protection against cold when sown and as a seedling in spring, and during the winter)
HP	hardy perennial (perennial that may be grown without special protection against cold)
lf	leaf
lvs	leaves
P	perennial (plant that continues to grow for a number of years)
perenn	alternative to above
Sp	species (singular)
Spp	species (plural)
Sps	alternative to above
Ssp	sub-species (singular)
Ssps	sub-species (plural)
Subsp	alternative to above abbreviation (singular)
var	variety

This section describes the principal symbols and conventions used in the Ordnance Survey 1:50,000 Second Series Maps of Great Britain.

The 1:50,000 scape maps replace the earlier one inch:one mile (1:63,360) maps — the change enabling the Ordnance Survey to include more detail and providing maps with a convenient metric scale (2cm to 1km). So that the new scale could be introduced reasonably quickly and uniformly, a 1:50,000 First Series was produced by photographic enlargement of the existing one inch:one mile maps. These First Series maps are gradually being replaced by maps to the Second Series specification. Most of the colours and symbols used for the First Series conform to the conventions employed in the Second Series.

ROADS, ROAD FEATURES, PATHS

Note: The different colours used for road symbols (or as colour infills to road symbols with black outlines) signify the following:

blue	motorway (multi-lane)
red	trunk or main road
orange	secondary road
yellow	tarred minor road
white	(ie no infill) untarred minor road or minor road in towns

Note: Except where stated otherwise, the symbols in this section do not necessarily imply public rights of way.

road

unfenced side to road; indicated by broken outline

dual carriageway

narrow road with passing places

road under construction

elevated road

gradient, 1 in 7 to 1 in 5

gradient, 1 in 5 and steeper

road tunnel

bridge

footbridge

gates

vehicle ferry

passenger ferry

service area

path (black) or **bridleway** with public right of way (red)

footpath with public right of way (red)

byway open to all traffic (red) or **road used as public path** (red)

Note: Public rights of way apply in England and Wales but not in Scotland.

RAILWAYS, RAILWAY FEATURES

multiple or single track

narrow-gauge track

freight line, siding or **tramway**

station; open station (red infill), station closed to passengers (white infill)

principal station (red infill)

CARTOGRAPHY 1

level crossing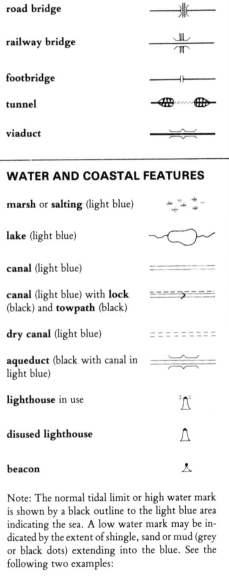

embankment

cutting

road bridge

railway bridge

footbridge

tunnel

viaduct

high and low water marks
(see note above)

shingle, mud or sand

GENERAL FEATURES

slope (arrowheads point
down slope)

cliffs (examples)

scree (dotted areas) below
cliff

outcrop of rock

quarry

spoil heap, refuse tip or
dump

wood (light green infill)

WATER AND COASTAL FEATURES

marsh or salting (light blue)

lake (light blue)

canal (light blue)

canal (light blue) with lock
(black) and towpath (black)

dry canal (light blue)

aqueduct (black with canal in
light blue)

lighthouse in use

disused lighthouse

beacon

Note: The normal tidal limit or high water mark
is shown by a black outline to the light blue area
indicating the sea. A low water mark may be indicated by the extent of shingle, sand or mud (grey
or black dots) extending into the blue. See the
following two examples:

normal tide limit
(see note above)

orchard (dark green dots)

park or ornamental grounds
(grey infill)

buildings (examples) (orange
tint infill)

public buildings (examples)
(heavy black outline, orange
tint infill)

ruin (white infill)

electricity transmission line
(with pylons spaced
conventionally)

pipe line (arrows indicate
direction of flow)

radio or TV mast

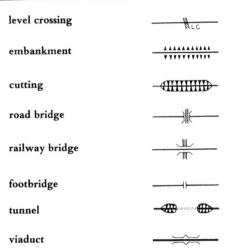

CARTOGRAPHY 1

church or chapel with tower	♠
church or chapel with spire	♠
church or chapel without tower or spire	+
chimney or tower	○
glasshouse	⬦
graticule intersections at 5' intervals (blue)	+
triangulation pillar (blue)	△
heliport	⊕
windmill with or without sails	⚚
windpump	⟊
Ministry of Defence ranges in area, indicating danger — observe warning notices (red letters)	Danger Area
Roman antiquity (example)	VILLA
non-Roman antiquity (example)	Castle
battlefield (with date)	✕
tumulus	∴
position of antiquity which cannot be drawn to scale	+
bus or coach station (red infill)	⬬
golfcourse or links	⌐
public telephone	✆
motoring organization telephone (blue)	✆
public convenience (in rural areas)	□ PC

TOURIST INFORMATION

information centre (blue)	ℹ
place of interest, beauty spot, place of historic interest, historic house, country park or ancient monument (blue)	▨
viewpoint (blue)	⛰
parking (blue)	P
picnic site (blue)	✕
camp site (blue)	⛺
caravan site (blue)	🚐
youth hostel (red)	▲

BOUNDARIES

national	— + — + —
county, region or islands area	— · — · —
London borough	○ — ○ — ○ — ○
district	— ▸ — ▸ — ▸ —
national park or forest park (yellow)	▬▬▬

HEIGHT

contours (example); contours are drawn in orange at 10m vertical intervals or, where standard metre contours are not available, at 50ft (15.24m) vertical intervals — with values given to the nearest metre

50

height (example); heights are given to the nearest metre above mean sea level

• 144

Note: Heights shown close to a triangulation pillar refer to the station height at ground level and not necessarily to the summit.

ABBREVIATIONS

CG	coastguard
CH	clubhouse

FC	Forestry Commission (red)
MP	milepost
MS	milestone
NT	National Trust (red if always open, blue if opening restricted)
NTS	National Trust for Scotland (red if always open, blue if opening restricted)
P	post office
PH	public house

This section describes the principal map symbols and conventions used in the Ordnance Survey 1:25,000 Second Series (metric) maps of Great Britain. Because of changes in specification some maps, issued as part of the series, contain certain conventions different to those given.

ROADS, ROAD FEATURES, PATHS

Note: Most types of road are coloured orange with black outlines; tarred minor roads generally less than 4m wide are coloured light orange with black outlines; untarred minor roads, minor roads in towns, drives and tracks are white with black outlines. Roads and tracks have dotted or broken outlines where unfenced. Except where stated otherwise, the symbols in this section do not necessarily imply public rights of way.

motorway

dual carriageway

road

minor road (untarred), minor road in towns, drive or track

path

footpath with public right of way (green)

bridlepath with public right of way (green)

road used as a public path or **byway open to all traffic** (green)

Note: The public rights of way indicated by the above three symbols apply in England and Wales but not in Scotland.

RAILWAYS, RAILWAY FEATURES

multiple track

single track

narrow gauge

siding

cutting

embankment

tunnel

road over

road under

level crossing

station (grey infill)

WATER AND COASTAL FEATURES

marsh (blue)

saltings (blue)

sand and shingle (black on light orange)

dunes (black on light orange)

Note: **Sand** is indicated by an area of light orange. **Mud** is indicated by an area of brown-grey.

example showing normal tidal limit, **mean low water** and **mean high water**. In tidal zones

light blue indicates the area covered by water at mean low water, while the mean high level of the water is indicated by a separate heavy blue line. The inter-tidal area is normally given a texture of colour to show the nature of the material (mud, sand, gravel, etc) to be found there.

lake (blue)		**sloping masonry**	
canal (blue)		**church or chapel with tower**	
lock		**church or chapel with spire**	
footbridge		**church or chapel without tower or spire**	+
ford		**triangulation point on churches or chapels**	
spring (blue)	Spr o	**building** (grey infill)	
well (blue)	W o	**glasshouse**	
beacon		**bus or coach station** (red infill)	
triangulation point on beacon		**chimney**	o
lighthouse		**triangulation point on chimney**	
triangulation point on lighthouse		**triangulation point on building**	
lightship		**triangulation station**	△

GENERAL FEATURES

slope (arrowheads point down slope)

cliff and rock features

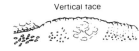

Vertical face

Loose rock Boulders Outcrop Scree

gravel pit

sand pit

disused pit or quarry

chalk or clay pit or quarry

refuse or slag heap

electricity transmission line supported by pylon

electricity transmission line supported by pole

Roman antiquity, AD 43 to AD 420 (example) — VILLA

non-Roman antiquity (example) — Castle

site of antiquity

site of battle (with date)

VEGETATION

coniferous trees (black on light green)

non-coniferous trees (black on light green)

coppice (black on light green)

orchard

CARTOGRAPHY 2

scrub

bracken

heath

rough grassland

Note: Bracken, heath and rough grassland are all shown as rough grassland on some maps.

reeds (blue)

BOUNDARIES

Note: Coincident boundaries are shown by the first appropriate symbol (below). For Ordnance Survey purposes, county boundary is deemed to be the limit of the parish structure whether or not a parish area adjoins.

county (England and Wales) or **region** or **island area** (Scotland)   — . — . — . —

district   — — — — —

London borough   -◇-◇-◇-◇-◇-◇-

civil parish (England) or **community** (Wales)   . . . .

constituency (county, borough or burgh)   — — — — — —

HEIGHT

contours (example); contours are generally at 5m vertical intervals but on some sheets are at 10m vertical intervals, and on others at 25ft vertical intervals (with values to the nearest metric equivalent) (orange)

90
75
65
60

height (example); determined by ground survey (black) or determined by air survey (orange)   50 ·

Note: Heights shown close to a triangulation pillar refer to the station height at ground level and not necessarily to the summit.

ABBREVIATIONS

A	AA telephone
BP	boundary post
BS	boundary stone
CH	club house
F	foot ferry
FB	footbridge
Ho	house
Mon	monument
MP	mile post
MS	mile stone
NT	National Trust (green if always open, blue if opening restricted)
NTS	National Trust for Scotland (green if always open, blue if opening restricted)
P	post office (rural area only)
PC	public convenience (rural area only)
PH	public house (rural area only)
R	RAC telephone
Sch	school
Spr	spring (blue)
T	public telephone
TH	town hall
Twr	tower
V	vehicle ferry
W	well (blue)
Wd Pp	wind pump
Y	youth hostel

CARTOGRAPHY 3

This section describes the principal topographic symbols used by the US Geological Survey (part of the United States Department of the Interior). The Geological Survey produces topographic maps of all parts of the United States and also of Puerto Rico, the (US) Virgin Islands, Guam, American Samoa and Antarctica. Various scales are used from 1:20,000 to 1:1,000,000 — certain areas being mapped at specific scales for historical or practical reasons.

Relief is indicated by contour lines and, on certain maps, by relief shading. Contour intervals vary as required by the nature of the terrain depicted and supplementary, dotted contours, at less than the regular interval, are used to describe selected flat areas.

Colours are used to depict the following:

black	man-made or cultural features (roads, buildings, names, boundaries)
blue	water or hydrographic features (lakes, rivers, canals, swamps, glaciers)
brown	relief
green	woodland (with patterns to show scrub, vineyards, orchards, etc)
red	to emphasize important roads and to show public land subdivision lines, land grants, fence and field lines,
red tint	urban areas in which only landmark buildings are shown
purple	office revisions from aerial photographs (ie changes that have not been field checked)

ROADS, ROAD FEATURES, PATHS

dual highway, dividing strip 25ft or less (red infill)

dual highway, dividing strip exceeding 25ft (red infill, white dividing strip)

primary highway with hard surface (red infill)

secondary highway with hard surface (red/white infill)

light-duty road with hard or improved surface

unimproved road

trail

road under construction, alignment known (red infill)

proposed road (red)

road bridge

footbridge

road drawbridge

road tunnel

road overpass and underpass

RAILROADS, RAILROAD FEATURES
(railway, railway features)

single track

multiple track

railroads in juxtaposition

narrow-gauge single track

narrow-gauge multiple track

railroad in street

carline

CARTOGRAPHY 3

railroad bridge	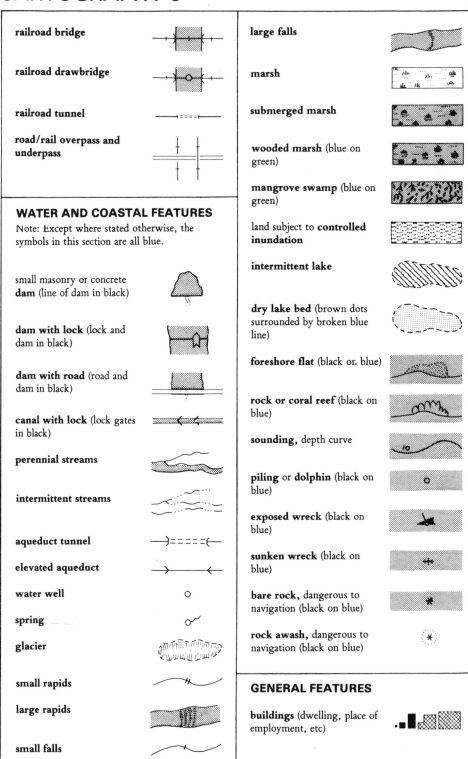
railroad drawbridge	
railroad tunnel	
road/rail overpass and underpass	

WATER AND COASTAL FEATURES

Note: Except where stated otherwise, the symbols in this section are all blue.

small masonry or concrete **dam** (line of dam in black)

dam with lock (lock and dam in black)

dam with road (road and dam in black)

canal with lock (lock gates in black)

perennial streams

intermittent streams

aqueduct tunnel

elevated aqueduct

water well

spring

glacier

small rapids

large rapids

small falls

large falls

marsh

submerged marsh

wooded marsh (blue on green)

mangrove swamp (blue on green)

land subject to **controlled inundation**

intermittent lake

dry lake bed (brown dots surrounded by broken blue line)

foreshore flat (black or. blue)

rock or coral reef (black on blue)

sounding, depth curve

piling or **dolphin** (black on blue)

exposed wreck (black on blue)

sunken wreck (black on blue)

bare rock, dangerous to navigation (black on blue)

rock awash, dangerous to navigation (black on blue)

GENERAL FEATURES

buildings (dwelling, place of employment, etc)

buildings (barn, warehouse, etc)

school

church

cemetery

Cem

alternative to above symbol

power transmission line with located metal tower

telephone line, pipeline, etc (labelled as to type)

wells other than water (labelled as to type)   ○ Oil   ○ Gas

tanks, oil, water, etc (labelled only if water)   ● ● ● ⊘ Water

located or landmark object   ○

windmill

open pit or **mine**

prospect   X

shaft

tunnel entrance   Y

mine dump (brown)

fill (brown with black road outline)

cut (brown with black railroad)

levee (brown)

levee with road (brown with black road outline)

wash (brown)

tailings (brown)

tailings pond (brown)

shifting sand or **dunes** (brown)

sand area (brown)

gravel beach (brown)

intricate surface (brown)

woods or **brushwood** (green)

Note: See *Water and Coastal Features* for *wooded marsh* and *mangrove swamp*

orchard (green)

vineyard (green)

scrub (green)

urban area (red tint)

BOUNDARIES

national

state

country, parish or **municipio**

civil township, precinct, town, barrio

incorporated city, village, hamlet

reservation, national or state

small park, cemetery, airport, etc

land grant (red)

CARTOGRAPHY 3

township or range line — United States land survey (red) _____

township or range line — approximate location (red) – – – – – – – –

section line — United States land survey (red) _____

section line — approximate location (red) – – – – – – – –

township line — not United States land survey (red) ....

section line — not United States land survey (red) ....

found corner: section and closing (red)

boundary monument, land grant (red) or other (black) □ . . . . □

fence or field line (red) – – – – – – – –

HEIGHT
including horizontal and vertical control stations (ie triangulation points and bench marks)

index contour (brown)

intermediate contour (brown)

supplementary contour (brown)

depression contour (brown)

horizontal and vertical control station; tablet, spirit level elevation — BM △ 5653

horizontal and vertical control station; other recoverable mark, spirit level elevation — △ 5455

horizontal control station; tablet, vertical angle elevation — VABM △ 95I9

horizontal control station; any recoverable mark, vertical angle or checked elevation — △3775

vertical control station; tablet, spirit level elevation — BM × 957

vertical control station; other recoverable mark, spirit level elevation — × 954

spot elevation (black or brown) — × 7369

water elevation (black or blue) — 670

CHEMISTRY

The letter symbols representing the elements are international. Certain of the element symbols are derived from the Latin names for chemical substances, eg K which represents potassium is derived from the word *kalium*. An element symbol may be used to represent one atom of an element or the substance which is comprised of these atoms. If an element symbol is used to represent more than one atom in a formula or description of a chemical compound, it is followed by a small figure giving the number of atoms it represents.

See also *Units of Measurement* and *Mathematics*.

THE ELEMENTS

Note: The following letter symbols are arranged in alphabetical order.

Ac	actinium	Fm	fermium
Ag	silver	Fr	francium
Al	aluminium		
Am	americium	Ga	gallium
Ar	argon	Gd	gadolinium
As	arsenic	Ge	germanium
At	astatine		
Au	gold	H	hydrogen
		He	helium
B	boron	Hf	hafnium
Ba	barium	Hg	mercury
Be	beryllium	Ho	holmium
Bi	bismuth		
Bk	berkelium	I	iodine
Br	bromine	In	indium
		Ir	iridium
C	carbon		
Ca	calcium	K	potassium
Cd	cadmium	Kr	krypton
Ce	cerium		
Cf	californium	La	lanthanum
Cl	chlorine	Li	lithium
Cm	curium	Lr	lawrencium
Co	cobalt	Lu	lutetium
Cr	chromium		
Cr	caesium	Md	mendelevium
Cu	copper	Mg	magnesium
		Mn	manganese
Dy	dysprosium	Mo	molybdenum
		N	nitrogen
Er	erbium	Na	sodium
Es	einsteinium	Nb	niobium
Eu	europium	Nd	neodymium
		Ne	neon
F	fluorine	Ni	nickel
Fe	iron	No	nobelium
Np	neptunium	Sm	samarium
		Sn	tin
O	oxygen	Sr	strontium
Os	osmium		
		Ta	tantalum
P	phosphorus	Tb	terbium
Pa	protactinium	Tc	technetium
Pb	lead	Te	tellurium
Pd	palladium	Th	thorium
Pm	promethium	Ti	titanium
Pr	praseodymium	Tl	thallium
Pt	platinum	Tm	thulium
Pu	plutonium		
		U	uranium
Ra	radium		
Rb	rubidium	V	vanadium
Re	rhenium		
Rh	rhodium	W	tungsten
Rn	radon		
Ru	ruthenium	Xe	xenon
S	sulphur	Y	yttrium
Sb	antimony	Yb	ytterbium
Sc	scandium		
Se	selenium	Zn	zinc
Si	silicon	Zr	zirconium

FORMULAS AND EQUATIONS

The **molecular formula** of a chemical compound gives the total number of atoms of each element contained in one molecule of the substance; eg

molecular formula for **water** (two hydrogen atoms and one oxygen atom) H_2O

The **constitutional formula** of any compound, as far as possible, expresses the arrangement as well as the number of atoms of each element in a molecule and, thereby, should normally distinguish it from any isomers (compounds with the

CHEMISTRY

same molecular formula but with different properties arising from different spatial arrangements of the atoms within a molecule); eg

the constitutional formula for **dimethyl ether** (see *structural formula* below) CH_3OCH_3

the constitutional formula for **ethyl alcohol** (see *structural formula* below) CH_3CH_2OH

brackets may be used to enclose any repeated group of elements within a formula. The bracketed group is normally followed by a small figure, in an inferior position, giving the number of repeats. The bracketed formula for the indefinitely repeated molecular structure of polymers (plastics) may be followed by the letter 'n'; eg   ()

hexamine $(CH_2)_6N_4$
$(CH_2CH_2CH_2CH_2CH_2CH_2N_4)$

polymer (polytetrafluoroethylene — 'Teflon') $(CF_2-CF_2)_n$

an **indefinite number** of (see *brackets* above)   n

a straight line is used to indicate a **valence bond** (chemical bond) between atoms in a compound's **structural formula** (ie a diagram of a molecule's arrangement of atoms and links between them); eg   —

the structural formula for **dimethyl ether**

$$\begin{array}{ccc} H & & H \\ | & & | \\ H-C-O-C-H \\ | & & | \\ H & & H \end{array}$$

the structural formula for **ethyl alcohol**

$$\begin{array}{ccc} H & & H \\ | & & | \\ H-C-C-O-H \\ | & & | \\ H & & H \end{array}$$

the structural formula for **acetylene** (see *electronic structure* below) $H-C\equiv C-H$

Note: Multiple bonds (as between the carbon atoms in the above example), although normally stronger than single bonds, do not imply a directly proportionally stronger link between the atoms.

benzene; the symbol implies a ring of carbon atoms, with each corner of the hexagon representing one carbon atom linked to a hydrogen atom. Various **benzene derivatives** or **homocyclic compounds** (ie those consisting of rings of only carbon atoms) may be indicated by this symbol marked with alternatives to the hydrogen atoms and/or linked groups of this symbol; eg

bromobenzene

phenanthrene; three benzene-type, carbon atom rings, each sharing two carbon atoms

alternative symbol for **benzene**

pyridine; example of a symbol for a **heterocyclic compound** (ie compound with a ring structure containing various elements) — each corner represents a carbon atom attached to a hydrogen atom, unless marked otherwise

The **electronic structure** of atoms may be indicated by their letter symbols followed by a series of figures: the first giving the number of electrons in the inner shell (ie the shell of electrons nearest the nucleus); the second, the number of electrons in the next outer shell, and so on; eg

the electronic structure of **magnesium**   Mg,2,8,2

Outer-shell electrons may be indicated by dots, small circles or crosses around an element symbol which then implies the remainder of the atom; eg

magnesium — see *electronic structure* above

$\overset{\displaystyle\cdot}{\underset{\displaystyle\cdot}{\text{Mg}}}$

acetylene — see *electronic structure* and *structural formula* above

H:C:::C:H

Note: Valence bonds are believed to be formed by the sharing or transfer of outer-shell electrons between atoms.

plus; symbol used as in examples of chemical equations below

$+$

positive, positively charged; symbol often used after item so charged

$+$

negative, negatively charged; symbol often used after item so charged

$-$

a little ('delta' — Greek, lower-case letter); symbol may be used with $+$ or $-$ to indicate a slight positive or negative charge

δ

becomes, reaction changes material on left of arrow (the reactants) to that on the right (the products); symbol used in chemical equations. Any condition, solvent-medium, catalyst, etc required for a described reaction to take place may be indicated above or below the arrow; eg

$\rightarrow$

example of a chemical **equation** (showing heat being required to form each molecule of carbon disulphide from one carbon and two sulphur atoms)

$C + 25 \xrightarrow{\text{heat}} CS_2$

equilibrium; used in chemical equations to imply a reversible reaction that continues in both directions and tends towards a stable state in which the rate of change of material on the left to that on the right equals the rate of change of material on the right to that on the left

$\rightleftharpoons$

released as a gas, 'given off'; used after item so affected; eg

$\uparrow$

equation showing the action of the yeast enzyme, zymase, on glucose to produce ethyl alcohol and carbon dioxide

$$C_6H_{12}O_6 \xrightarrow{\text{zymase}} 2C_2H_5OH + CO_2\uparrow$$

precipitated, insoluble solid formed from out of a solution; used after symbol for compound precipitated

$\downarrow$

a **full-stop** or a **comma** may be used to separate a molecular formula from a number followed by the molecular formula for water. The number then indicates the number of water molecules taken up for each molecule of the compound on crystallization (should only one water molecule be so taken up, the number may be omitted); eg

. ,

sodium carbonate crystallizes as **decahydrate**

$Na_2CO_3.10H_2O$

an **electron;** commonly used in representations of reactions such as electrolysis

e

normal temperature and pressure; ie O°C and 1 atmosphere

N.T.P.

standard temperature and pressure; is O°C and 1 atmosphere

S.T.P.

normal; used in reference to the concentration of a compound in a solution; ie the equivalent weight of substance dissolved in one litre

N

optical isomers (compounds which have identical constitutional formulas but different spatial arrangements) may sometimes be distinguished by one of the letters 'D' and 'L' or 'R' and 'S' used in front of the compound's name

D,L
R,S

COMMERCE

The following symbols may be found in accounts, quotations and other forms of commercial documentation in English speaking countries. See also *Money, Mathematics, Units of Measurement.*

at or at the rate of	@	**on account**	º/ₐ
account, account of	ᵃ/c	**correct** quotation (mainly used in USA)	✳
alternative to above symbol	A/c		
brought forward	ᵇ/f	**per**	℔
alternative to above symbol	ᵇ/fwd	alternative to above symbol	℔
carried down	ᵇ/d	**number** or item (mainly used in USA)	#
brought down	ᵇ/d	**none,** zero	—
carried forward	ᶜ/f	**per cent,** per hundred, hundredths of a whole	%
alternative to above symbol	ᶜ/fwd		
care of	ᶜ/o	**per thousand,** thousandths of a whole	‰

DATA PROCESSING 1

The following symbols represent processes or data and are linked by lines to form diagrams showing sequence of operations and flow of information. They are used to produce program flow charts (primarily the sequence of operations in a computer program) and data flow charts (showing the sequence of operations and the data involved — usually a diagram of a complete data processing system). Flow charts are typically drawn in hierachical groups, with one flow chart providing an outline of a whole system and references to the first of a series of lower levels of flow charts, each level giving progressively more detail of particular portions of the system requiring detailed description.

The normal direction of flow of data is from left to right or from top to bottom. Should the flow be different, or require clarification, it is indicated by arrows incorporated into the links.

Text can be included within a symbol to detail the function.

The following symbols are in accordance with BS 4058:1973 and, apart from the symbols for *off-page connector* and *control document,* they conform with ISO/R 1028.

For an alternative method of describing data processing systems, see *Data Processing-Structure Diagrams* below.

PROCESS SYMBOLS

process, any form of processing; except in equipment-oriented flow charts where it is specifically computer processing

decision, operation determining which of a number of alternative routes are to be taken

preparation, modification of instruction(s); eg setting a switch

predefined process, named process or sub-routine described elsewhere

manual operation, off-line operation at manual speed

auxiliary operation, off-line operation on equipment not directly controlled by main unit

merge, combining two or more sets of data into one set

extract, removing one or more sets from one set

collate, forming two or more sets from two or more different sets

sort, arrange set of items into a specific sequence

DATA PROCESSING 1

DATA SYMBOLS

input-output, any equipment/process introducing into or producing data from the system

Note: The following 14 symbols are not used in program flow charts.

document input-output

punched card input-output (also mark-sense card, stub-card, mark-scan card, etc)

deck of cards, collection of punched cards

file of cards

paper tape input-output

display, any means of displaying information during processing (using printers, VDU screens, etc)

manual input using buttons, keyboard, etc

control document, ie tally roll audit tape, batch control data, etc

on-line storage — eg magnetic tape or disk

magnetic tape input-output

magnetic drum input-output

magnetic disk input-output

processor storage input-output

off-line storage

LINKS/FLOW LINES

parallel mode; used to show start and end of one or more simultaneous operations (not used in program flow charts)

telecommunication link (not used in program flow charts)

crossing of flow lines; no interaction or connection between them is indicated

junction of flow lines; all such junctions are staggered to avoid confusion with crossing lines (see above)

connector, indicator of exit to or entry from another section of a flow chart

off-page connector, alternative to connector (above) for use from one page to another

terminal/interrupt, start, stop, delay point in flow chart

SYMBOL IDENTIFICATION/CROSS REFERENCES

striped symbol (example); character code in stripe of symbol (above) provides identification of cross reference to more detailed representation of process (below)

X X5

symbol identifier (example); symbols are identified by characters above and to the left of each symbol

M M

symbol cross reference (example); note group of characters above and to right of symbol giving a reference to an additional explanation of that part of system

M M

annotation; indicator of explanatory notes

Data processing systems and programs may be described or analysed by the use of structure diagrams as an alternative to, or together with, *Flow Charts* (see above). A structure diagram consists of a hierarchic series of elements: the top element describes or names the process overall and is linked to elements beneath which describe the process in progressively greater detail.

The symbols for structure diagrams have not been standardized to the same extent as those for flow charts and variations may be found, particularly in the means employed to indicate 'no action', possible points of exit and entry, and links between boxes and diagram sheets. Normally, as in the system shown below, each element is contained in a box and, unless marked otherwise, each row of boxes describes the charted process, part by part, sequentially from left to right — with the first part of the process in the first box and so on.

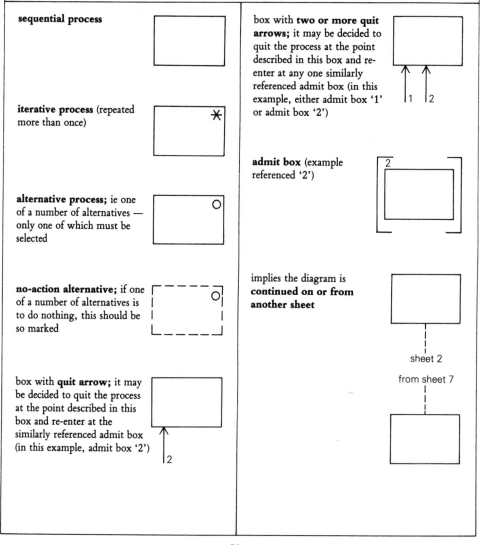

sequential process

iterative process (repeated more than once)

alternative process; ie one of a number of alternatives — only one of which must be selected

no-action alternative; if one of a number of alternatives is to do nothing, this should be so marked

box with **quit arrow**; it may be decided to quit the process at the point described in this box and re-enter at the similarly referenced admit box (in this example, admit box '2')

box with **two or more quit arrows**; it may be decided to quit the process at the point described in this box and re-enter at any one similarly referenced admit box (in this example, either admit box '1' or admit box '2')

admit box (example referenced '2')

implies the diagram is **continued on or from another sheet**

sheet 2

from sheet 7

simple example of the use of
the principal symbols showing
method of linking

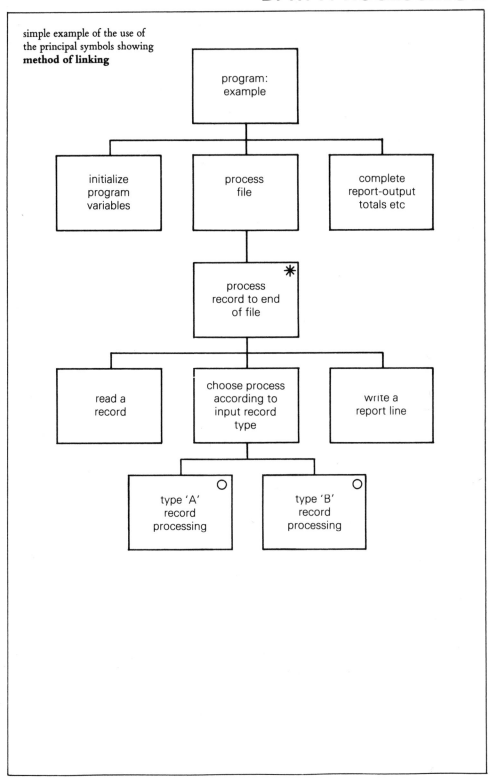

The following symbols are used for architectural and installation plans and diagrams. Except where stated otherwise, they conform with the recommendations of the International Electrotechnical Commission. In general the IEC's symbols have been adopted in Europe (including Great Britain) and are widely used elsewhere. The source of the following IEC symbols has been BS 3939: Section 27 'Graphical Symbols for Electrical, Power, Telecommunications and Electronics Diagrams'.

Symbols other than those recommended by the IEC have been given where there is no available relevant IEC symbol or an alternative symbol is in common use; and these have been marked 'not IEC'.

American standard electrical symbols differ considerably from those used in Europe — see *Electrical 2*. See *Electronics* for symbols for electronic components.

WIRING

wiring, general symbol

wiring on the surface

wiring under the surface

wiring in conduit

wiring in duct or trunking

wiring going upwards

wiring going downwards

vertical wire through room

joint or junction box; example with three outlets; for a joint box a dot is shown at the connection

SWITCHES AND BUTTONS

single-pole, one-way switch (a number of switches at one point may be indicated)

one-way switch (not IEC), commonly used alternative to above symbol (GB)

two-pole, one-way switch

cord-operated single-pole, one way switch

two-way switch

two-way switch (not IEC), commonly used alternative to above symbol (GB)

intermediate switch

switch with **pilot lamp**

period limiting switch

regulating switch eg dimmer

push button

luminous push button

restricted access push button

(restricted access) **push button for fire alarm**

key-operated switch or watchman system device

DISTRIBUTION AND CONTROL UNITS

main control unit (not IEC), in common use (GB)

disribution board or point; note the circuit controlled by the board may be indicated by the addition of an appropriate qualifying symbol; eg distribution board **for lighting circuits**

isolator, main or sub-main switch (not IEC), in common use (GB)

integrating meter, the inserted letters indicate the measured quantity (example shown is a watt-hour meter)

starter

transformer, general symbol (note BS 3939:Section 6 gives alternative symbols for specific forms of transformer)

thermostat, block symbol (not IEC — conforms with BS 3939:Section 27)

time switch

SOCKET OUTLETS

socket outlets (mains); general symbol; in GB this normally implies the presence of an earthing contact — exceptions should be annotated, eg shaver outlet

switched socket outlet

switched socket outlet (not IEC), in common use (GB)

socket outlet **with interlocking switch**

multiple socket outlet (example shown for three plugs)

LIGHTING

lighting point or lamp, general symbol; the number, power and type of light should be specified

ceiling-mounted lighting fitting (not IEC), commonly used alternative to above symbol (GB)

wall-mounted lighting point or lamp

wall-mounted lighting fitting (not IEC), commonly used alternative to above symbol (GB)

emergency (safety) lighting point

switched lighting point, ie with built-in switch

variable lamp, ie fed from variable voltage supply

ELECTRICAL 1

lamp with reflector or a projector	
spotlight	
single fluorescent lamp	
group of **three fluorescent** lamps	
group of **three fluorescent** lamps; example of simplified version of above	
discharge lamp lighting outlet (not IEC), in common use (GB)	
auxiliary apparatus for discharge lamp, used only when auxiliary apparatus is separate from lamp fixture	
illuminated sign, symbol is annotated as required; may include arrow to imply direction	

Note: The above symbol may also be used combined with the symbol for an emergency lighting point to indicate an illuminated **emergency or safety sign.**

signal lamp	

ELECTRICAL APPLIANCES

electrical appliance, general symbol	
fan, or 'ventilating' (when used to label distribution board)	
heater (type should be specified) or 'heating' (when used to label distribution board)	

heater (not IEC), alternative to above symbol (GB)	
motor	
motor (not IEC), alternative to above symbol (GB)	
generator	

COMMUNICATION EQUIPMENT
including telephone

telephone point (not IEC); used as general telephone or telephone point symbol or as **external** telephone point symbol, if an internal symbol is also shown	
internal telephone point or telephone	
manual switchboard	
automatic telephone exchange equipment	
telecommunication socket outlet, normally qualified with appropriate initials; eg **television socket outlet**	
teleprinter	
aerial	

amplifier	
microphone	
loudspeaker	

OTHER ITEMS

automatic fire detector

bell	
indicator panel (N = the number of ways)	N
clock	
master clock	
earth	

The following symbols are used for architectural and electrical installation plans and diagrams in the USA. Except where stated otherwise, they conform with ANSI Y32.9: 1972.

For symbols used in Europe see previous section: *Electrical 1*. See *Electronics* for symbols for electronic components.

WIRING AND DUCTS

Note: Heavy lines are used to identify service and feed runs.

wiring concealed in ceiling or wall

wiring concealed in floor

wiring exposed

homerun to panel board; the number of arrows indicates the number of circuits.

Any circuit without identification indicates a two-wire circuit. Greater numbers of wires are indicated by an appropriate number of cross-lines; eg

three wires

wiring turned up

wiring turned down

underfloor duct and junction box for triple, double or single duct system as implied by the number of parallel lines

cellular floor header duct

trolley duct

busway (service, feeder or plug-in)

wireway

SWITCHES AND BUTTONS

single-pole switch   **S**

key-operated switch   **S**K

Note: A number of switch types are indicated by the symbol for a single-pole switch suffixed by the following letters (in a similar manner to the key-operated switch symbol above):

CB   circuit breaker switch
D   door switch
L   switch for low-voltage switching system
LM   master switch for low-voltage switching system
MC   momentary contact switch or push button for other signalling system
P   switch and pilot light
T   time switch

switch and single receptacle

switch and double receptacle

ceiling pull switch

push-button station (general symbol)

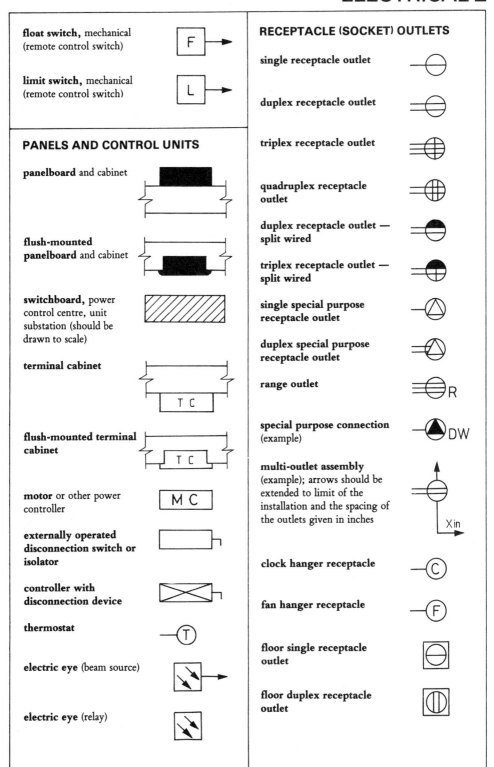

float switch, mechanical (remote control switch)

limit switch, mechanical (remote control switch)

PANELS AND CONTROL UNITS

panelboard and cabinet

flush-mounted panelboard and cabinet

switchboard, power control centre, unit substation (should be drawn to scale)

terminal cabinet

flush-mounted terminal cabinet

motor or other power controller

externally operated disconnection switch or isolator

controller with disconnection device

thermostat

electric eye (beam source)

electric eye (relay)

RECEPTACLE (SOCKET) OUTLETS

single receptacle outlet

duplex receptacle outlet

triplex receptacle outlet

quadruplex receptacle outlet

**duplex receptacle outlet —
split wired**

**triplex receptacle outlet —
split wired**

single special purpose receptacle outlet

duplex special purpose receptacle outlet

range outlet

special purpose connection (example)

multi-outlet assembly (example); arrows should be extended to limit of the installation and the spacing of the outlets given in inches

clock hanger receptacle

fan hanger receptacle

floor single receptacle outlet

floor duplex receptacle outlet

ELECTRICAL 2

Note: All the above receptacle outlets should be grounded (earthed) unless marked otherwise. The following abbreviations are used adjacent to the symbols to describe further the outlet type:

DT	dust-tight
EP	explosion-tight
G	grounded
R	recessed
RT	rain-tight
UNG	ungrounded
VT	vapour-tight
WP	waterproof
WT	watertight

floor telephone outlet — public

floor telephone outlet — private

Note: For other telephone outlets see *Institutional, Commercial and Industrial Occupancies* and *Residential Signalling System Devices* below.

LIGHTING OUTLETS

ceiling-mounted incandescent mercury-vapour or similar lamp fixture (surface or pendant)

wall-mounted incandescent mercury-vapour or similar lamp fixture (surface or pendant)

Note: Further types of wall- or ceiling-mounted fittings can be indicated by any of the following abbreviations being written within the above symbols as appropriate:

B	blanked outlet
J	junction box
L	outlet controlled by low-voltage switching when relay is installed in outlet box
R	recessed fitting
RX	recessed exit light
X	exit light

individual fluorescent fixture (surface or pendant)

recessed individual fluorescent fixture

continuous fluorescent fixture

(surface or pendant)

bare-lamp fluorescent strip

INSTITUTIONAL, COMMERCIAL AND INDUSTRIAL OCCUPANCIES

nurse call system device

paging system device

fire alarm system device

staff register system device

electric clock system device

public telephone system device

private telephone system device

Note: For floor telephone outlets see *Receptacle (Socket) Outlets* above.

watchman system device

sound system device

any other signal system device	

Note: Numbers given within the above symbols designate specific forms of the devices.

RESIDENTIAL SIGNALLING SYSTEM DEVICES

push-button

buzzer

bell

bell-buzer combination

annunciator

outside telephone

interconnecting telephone

Note: For floor telephone outlets see *Receptacle (Socket) Outlets above.*

general symbol

left blank this symbol implies an interconnection box. Letters written within this symbol give it the following meanings:

BT	bell-ringing transformer
CH	chime
D	electric door opener
M	maid's signal plug
R	radio outlet
TV	television outlet

UNDERGROUND ELECTRICAL DISTRIBUTION

manhole

handhole

transformer manhole or **vault**

transformer pad

underground cable (direct burial)

underground duct line

street light standard fed from underground circuit

AERIAL ELECTRICAL DISTRIBUTION

pole

streetlight and bracket

transformer

primary circuit

secondary circuit

down guy

head guy

sidewalk guy

service weather head

ELECTRONICS

Electronic diagrams are drawn to explain or record the details and wiring of electronic devices. Such diagrams primarily represent the functioning of electronic circuitry rather than the physical appearance of wires and components. In general, conductors are drawn as straight horizontal and vertical lines. Although like symbols should be drawn to the same size, their sizes need not relate to the actual size of the components represented; nor need a symbol's location directly relate to the physical location of the component represented. Wherever a diagram contains a clear sequence of cause and effect, this sequence should be shown from left to right and/or from top to bottom. If such a sequential arrangement is impractical, the direction of cause to effect should be indicated by an arrow. Components that operate simultaneously (eg are ganged together) may be shown linked by a dotted line.

The principal methods of providing location references to components within a diagram are by a grid reference system or by a tabular method. When a grid reference system is used, the diagram is regarded as divided by a grid of numbered (and/or lettered) vertical and horizontal lines and any component's location may be indicated by the numbers or letters of the lines forming the rectangle containing it. However, the grid lines themselves may frequently have to be omitted to avoid confusion with lines representing conductors. In the tabular method, a table is provided along the top or bottom of the drawing, with component references arranged vertically in line with the corresponding symbols. Normally designations are arranged in separate rows for different types of component; eg one row for capacitors, one for resistors and so on.

Binary logic element symbols are used in the design of systems using integrated circuits. Binary integrated circuits process and carry information in the form of two alternative states. Normally these two states are denoted by '0' and '1' and, in reality, are signalled by minimum and maximum voltages. Except when disconnected, these circuits never remain in any intermediate state.

Block symbols represent complete items of electronic equipment. They are used where only the basic electronic arrangement of linked devices needs to be shown. Where there is no block symbol for a particular item, other electronic symbols may be incorporated into the block diagrams or a description written within the square or rectangle representing the item. Generally, linking lines in block diagrams imply signal paths — power supply lines, if given, are normally shown separately.

Because of the wide and constantly changing range of electronic components in existence, it has been possible only to include a representative selection from the correspondingly wide range of electronic symbols. However, many electronic symbols are formed by the modification of symbolic elements or the addition of supplementary symbols to a basic symbol, and so it should be possible to deduce a meaning for most electronic symbols in current use from the ones given below.

Except where stated otherwise, the following symbols conform with the recommendations of the International Electrotechnical Commission which have been widely incorporated into national standards in Europe, America and elsewhere (the relevant British standard being BS 3939, while the US standards are ANSI Y32.2 (IEEE std 315-1975) and ANSI 32.14 (IEE std 91-1973). Where symbols are marked as US or

ELECTRONICS

British alternatives this does not necessarily preclude the use of IEC versions in those countries, as generally the IEC versions are equally acceptable in current practice.

All the IEC symbols in this section, including the binary logic circuit symbols, may be used in conjunction with each other and with appropriate electrical installation symbols – see *Electrical (International 1 and 2)*.

CONDUCTORS
including groups of conductors and conductor cross-overs and connections

conductor or group of conductors, general symbol. A line for a particular path (eg common chassis or earth lines) may be emphasized by increasing its thickness.

flexible conductor; used where it is especially required for the conductor to be flexible

jumper (cross or temporary connection)

two conductors

two conductors; single-line representation

three conductors

three conductors; single-line representation

multi-line (example showing eight conductors); should be drawn in groups of three lines

multi-line (example showing eight conductors); single-line representaton (the cross-stroke may be omitted if meaning is clear)

crossing conductors with no electrical connection

junction of conductors

double junction with two (vertically in line) conductors joined to one horizontal conductor. Note junction drawn staggered to avoid confusion with *crossing conductors* above.

alternative to above symbol

common point junction (example showing three conductors joined to a common line)

SUPPLEMENTARY SYMBOLS TO CONDUCTORS

twisting of conductors, general symbol

two conductors twisted

group of twisted conductors (example showing four conductors twisted out of seven)

cable, general symbol

three conductors in cable

61

ELECTRONICS

screening of conductor(s), general symbol

two conductors within a screen

example showing five **screened conductors** (including two individually screened) in a seven-conductor cable and with all screens being earthed

coaxial cable (wire with conductive sheath or screen), general symbol

ends of coaxial structure (example) with one end of outer sheath connected to a terminal

TERMINALS including earths

terminal or tag, general symbol

twin tag, eg two wires terminated in a twin screw terminal block

link normally closed with two readily separable contacts

earth

noiseless (clean) earth

chassis or **frame connection**

PLUGS AND SOCKETS

plug (male)

socket (female)

jack sleeve (bush)

jack spring

example of use of jack symbols — **three-pole concentric plug and jack**

SWITCHES

make-contact switch (normally open), general symbol

ganged switches (example showing two ganged make-contact switches)

alternative to **make-contact switch** above

break-contact switch (normally closed), general symbol

alternative to above symbol

changeover contact — break before make

changeover contact — make before break; note special shape of wiper typical of make before break switches

make-contact push button

break-contact push button

US version of above symbol

cam-operated changeover contact-unit (British version)

locking press button (plunger-type) key with two changeover contact-units (British version)

selector level with bridging wiper (make before break)

US alternative to above symbol

selector magnet operating coil of a selector

US and British alternative to above symbol

telegraph key, simple (US version)

morse key (British version)

RESISTORS AND POTENTIOMETERS
including heating elements

fixed resistor, general symbol

US and British alternative to above symbol

variable resistor

US and British alternative to above symbol

resistor with preset adjustment

US and British alternative to above symbol

fixed resistor with fixed tapping, voltage divider

US and British alternative to above symbol

voltage divider with moving contact, potentiometer or rheostat with variable voltage or resistance take-off from the slider (ie the arrow)

US and British alternative to above symbol

voltage divider with preset adjustment

US and British alternative to above symbol

resistor with pronounced positive resistance-temperature coefficient, eg ballast resistor or barretter

US and British alternative to above symbol

thermister or resistor with a pronounced negative resistance-temperature coefficient

US and British alternative to above symbol

heating element

US and British alternative to above symbol

CAPACITORS

capacitor, general symbol

ELECTRONICS

feed-through capacitor, ie a capacitor made from a feed-through device mounted in a chassis or other metal plate

polarized electrolytic capacitor, plus (+) sign may be omitted if meaning is clear

non-polarized electrolytic capacitor

variable capacitor

capacitor with preset adjustment

variable differential capacitor where $c_1 + c_2$ = constant

variable split-stator capacitor where $c_1 = c_2$

INDUCTORS, TRANSFORMERS AND TRANSDUCERS

Note: Many configurations of the winding and core symbols are used to depict the great range of inductive components in use. The core symbols imply ferromagnetic cores unless otherwise indicated.

winding, general symbol

alternative to above symbol

US and British alternatives to above two symbols

inductor with core

magnetic core of inductor or transformer (US only)

magnetic memory core (US only)

variable inductor

inductor with preset adjustment

transformer, general symbol

transformer, general symbol — simplified form

transformer with gap in ferromagnetic core

screen between transformer windings

single-phase autotransformer

RELAYS
including relay contact units

Note: The American National Standards Institute and the (American) Institute of Electrical and Electronics Engineers recommend use of the relay coil general symbol, alternating current relay coil symbol, slow-operating relay coil and the two non-IEC (US only) relay symbols with the following abbreviations.

AC	alternating current or ringing relay
D	differential
DB	double-based (biased in both directions)
DP	dashpot
EP	electrically polarized
FO	fast-operate
FR	fast-release

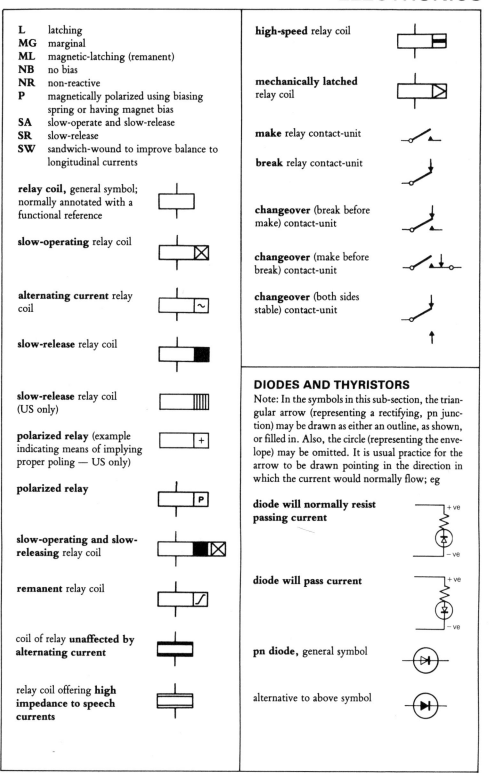

L latching
MG marginal
ML magnetic-latching (remanent)
NB no bias
NR non-reactive
P magnetically polarized using biasing spring or having magnet bias
SA slow-operate and slow-release
SR slow-release
SW sandwich-wound to improve balance to longitudinal currents

relay coil, general symbol; normally annotated with a functional reference

slow-operating relay coil

alternating current relay coil

slow-release relay coil

slow-release relay coil (US only)

polarized relay (example indicating means of implying proper poling — US only)

polarized relay

slow-operating and slow-releasing relay coil

remanent relay coil

coil of relay **unaffected by alternating current**

relay coil offering **high impedance to speech currents**

high-speed relay coil

mechanically latched relay coil

make relay contact-unit

break relay contact-unit

changeover (break before make) contact-unit

changeover (make before break) contact-unit

changeover (both sides stable) contact-unit

DIODES AND THYRISTORS

Note: In the symbols in this sub-section, the triangular arrow (representing a rectifying, pn junction) may be drawn as either an outline, as shown, or filled in. Also, the circle (representing the envelope) may be omitted. It is usual practice for the arrow to be drawn pointing in the direction in which the current would normally flow; eg

diode will normally resist passing current

diode will pass current

pn diode, general symbol

alternative to above symbol

ELECTRONICS

tunnel diode		**pnip transistor** with ohmic connection to the i region	
unidirectional breakdown diode, voltage reference diode, eg Zener diode		**pnin transistor** with ohmic connection to the i region	
bidirectional breakdown diode, eg clipper diode			
bidirectional diode, varistor		**JUGFET** (junction-gate field-effect transistor) — with n-type channel	
thyristor, general symbol		**JUGFET** (junction-gate field-effect transistor) — with p-type channel	
reverse-conducting diode thyristor		**IGFET** (insulated-gate field-effect transistor) — depletion-type with n-channel	
bidirectional diode thyristor		**IGFET** (insulated-gate field-effect transistor) — depletion-type with p-channel	
bidirectional triode thyristor or triac		**IGFET** (insulated-gate field-effect transistor) — depletion-type with substrate internally connected to emitter	

TRANSISTORS

pnp transistor (also pnip transistor if omission of the intrinsic region will not result in ambiguity)		**IGFET** (insulated-gate field effect transistor) — depletion-type, single-gate, p-channel, with external connection to substrate	
npn transistor with collector connected to envelope		**IGFET** (insulated-gate field-effect transistor) — depletion-type, two-gate, n-channel, with external connection to substrate	
npn avalanche transistor		**IGFET** (insulated-gate field-effect transistor) — enhancement-type, single-gate, p-channel, with external connection to substrate	
unijunction transistor with p-type base		**IGFET** (insulated-gate field-effect transistor) — enhancement-type, two gate, n-channel, with external connection to substrate	
unijunction transistor with n-type base			

THERMIONIC VALVES AND COLD CATHODE TUBES

including triodes, pentodes, cold cathode gas-charge tubes, cathode ray tubes and camera tubes

Note: Because of the large number of valves and tube types, only the basic symbol elements and commonest valve and tube types are given below. Other types are indicated by addition or variation of symbol elements.

filament, ie directly heated cathode or heater for indirectly heated cathode — symbol element

cathode (indirectly heated) — symbol element

anode — symbol element

grid or mesh (including control grid, screen grid, suppressor grid, etc) — symbol element

cold cathode (or ionically heated cathode) — symbol element

double diode (in one envelope)

triode, directly heated

tetrode, indirectly heated, with beam-forming electrode internally connected to cathode

pentode, indirectly heated, with diode internally connected to suppressor grid

triode hexode, indirectly heated
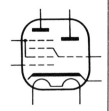

cold cathode discharge tube

multiple-diode cold cathode display tube (example)
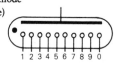

cold cathode discharge lamp (eg neon lamp)

Note: Symbols for cold cathode indicator or display tubes may contain more display letters or numbers and/or contain more than one cold cathode element symbol.

single-beam cathode ray tube, with two pairs of lateral electrostatic deflecting electrodes, three focusing electrodes (one cylindrical), intensity modulating electrode, cathode and heater — ie example of cathode ray tube as used in an oscilloscope
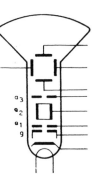

ELECTRONICS

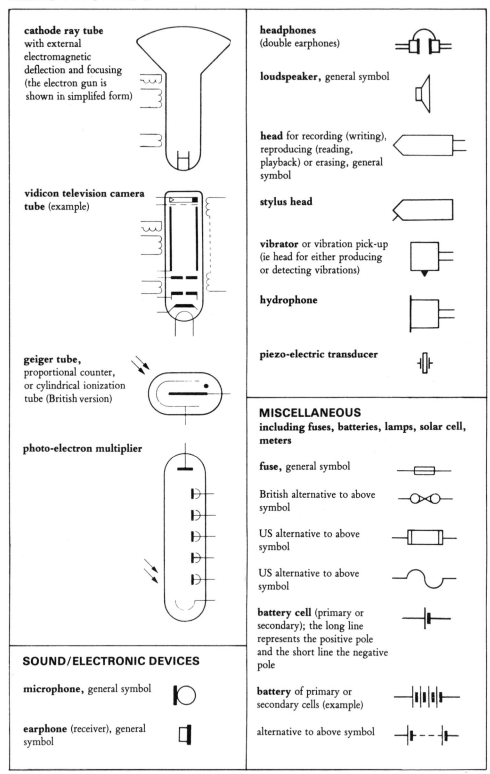

cathode ray tube with external electromagnetic deflection and focusing (the electron gun is shown in simplifed form)

vidicon television camera tube (example)

geiger tube, proportional counter, or cylindrical ionization tube (British version)

photo-electron multiplier

SOUND/ELECTRONIC DEVICES

microphone, general symbol

earphone (receiver), general symbol

headphones (double earphones)

loudspeaker, general symbol

head for recording (writing), reproducing (reading, playback) or erasing, general symbol

stylus head

vibrator or vibration pick-up (ie head for either producing or detecting vibrations)

hydrophone

piezo-electric transducer

MISCELLANEOUS
including fuses, batteries, lamps, solar cell, meters

fuse, general symbol

British alternative to above symbol

US alternative to above symbol

US alternative to above symbol

battery cell (primary or secondary); the long line represents the positive pole and the short line the negative pole

battery of primary or secondary cells (example)

alternative to above symbol

permanent magnet	]
rectifier	
signal lamp	
filament lamp	

Note: See *Thermionic Valves and Cold Cathode Tubes* above for neon lamp.

light-emitting diode (l.e.d.)	
solar cell or other photo-voltaic cell	
hall generator with four ohmic connections	
meter, indicating or measuring instrument, general symbol; used encircling the following symbols and letters; eg	◯
ammeter	(A)
ammeter*	A
current direction indicator	±
differential voltmeter	V-V
double voltmeter	∀
frequency meter	f
frequency meter	Hz
US alternative to above symbol *	F
galvanometer*	↑
ohmeter	Ω
US alternative to above symbol *	OHM
oscillograph (US only)*	OSCG

oscilloscope	
alternative to above symbol	OSC
phasemeter	φ
US alternative to above symbol *	PH
power factor meter	COSφ
US alternative to above symbol *	PF
pyrometer, thermometer	t°
salinity meter	NaCl
synchroscope	SYN
alternative to above symbol	
US alternative to above symbol *	SY
tachometer	n
varmeter*	var
voltmeter*	V
wattmeter*	W
wavemeter	λ

Note: Only the items marked with an asterisk (*) are in general use in the USA. For symbols for integrating meters see *Electrical I.*

GENERAL SUPPLEMENTARY SYMBOLS
Note: The symbols in this section are used in combination with other electronic symbols to augment or qualify their meaning.

positive polarity	+
negative polarity	–
magnetic field dependence (semi-conductor device) or **erasing** (sound recording device)	×

ELECTRONICS

light or other radiation; arrows pointing towards symbol indicate light-operated device, arrows pointing away indicate light-emitting and/or modulating device. The arrows are always drawn outside the symbol envelope.

temperature dependence

capacitor or capacitive effect

gas-filled envelope (indicated by black dot), as in cathode tubes

recording or reproducing; arrow points in direction of energy transfer (sound/ electronic device)

recording and reproducing, radiating and receiving (sound/electronic device)

magneto-striction type (sound/electronic device)

moving coil or ribbon type (sound/electronic device)

moving iron type (sound/electronic device)

stereo type (sound/electronic device)

low audio frequencies

high audio frequencies

disk (sound/electronic device)

tape or film (sound/electronic device)

drum (sound/electronic device)

BLOCK SYMBOLS

equipment, general symbol

non-rotating generator, general symbol

sine-wave generator (non-rotating)

sawtooth generator (non-rotating)

pulse generator (non-rotating)

variable frequency sine-wave generator (non-rotating)

noise generator (non-rotating)

changer, general symbol

rectifier

inverter

DC converter

frequency changer

frequency multiplier

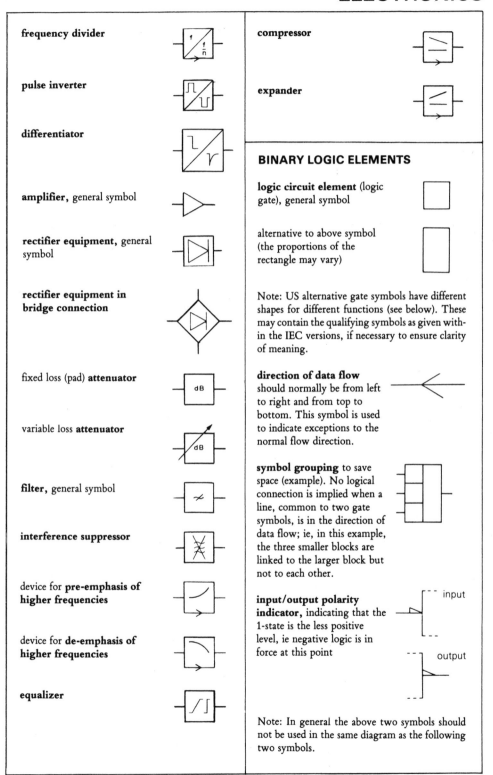

frequency divider

pulse inverter

differentiator

amplifier, general symbol

rectifier equipment, general symbol

rectifier equipment in bridge connection

fixed loss (pad) attenuator

variable loss attenuator

filter, general symbol

interference suppressor

device for pre-emphasis of higher frequencies

device for de-emphasis of higher frequencies

equalizer

compressor

expander

BINARY LOGIC ELEMENTS

logic circuit element (logic gate), general symbol

alternative to above symbol (the proportions of the rectangle may vary)

Note: US alternative gate symbols have different shapes for different functions (see below). These may contain the qualifying symbols as given within in the IEC versions, if necessary to ensure clarity of meaning.

direction of data flow should normally be from left to right and from top to bottom. This symbol is used to indicate exceptions to the normal flow direction.

symbol grouping to save space (example). No logical connection is implied when a line, common to two gate symbols, is in the direction of data flow; ie, in this example, the three smaller blocks are linked to the larger block but not to each other.

input/output polarity indicator, indicating that the 1-state is the less positive level, ie negative logic is in force at this point

input

output

Note: In general the above two symbols should not be used in the same diagram as the following two symbols.

ELECTRONICS

logic negated input/ output, indicating the state of the logic variable is reversed at the input

input

output

Note: The data-flow line may be drawn through the circles in the above two symbols.

inhibiting input; when standing at its 1-state, prevents a 1-output (or a 0-output if the output is negated) whatever the state of the other input variables

negated inhibiting input; when standing at its 0-state, prevents a 1-output (or a 0-output if the output is negated)

input or output **not carrying logic information**

AND gate; produces a 1-output if, and only if, all inputs are 1-inputs

US alternative to above symbol

NAND gate (AND with negated output); produces a 0-output, if and only if, all inputs are 1-inputs

US alternative to above symbol

OR gate; produces a 1-output if, and only if, one or more of its inputs are 1-inputs

US alternative to above symbol

exclusive OR gate; produces a 1-output only if one, and only one, of its inputs is a 1-input.

US alternative to above symbol

NOR gate; produces a 0-output if, and only if, one or more inputs are 1-inputs

US alternative to above symbol

logic identity gate; produces a 1-output if, and only if, all inputs are the same

wired connection where a number of elements are wired together to achieve the effect of an AND or an OR operation without the use of an explicit element

wire AND connection

alternative to above symbol

amplifier for logic diagrams (triangular symbol used within a square or rectangular logic circuit element symbol)

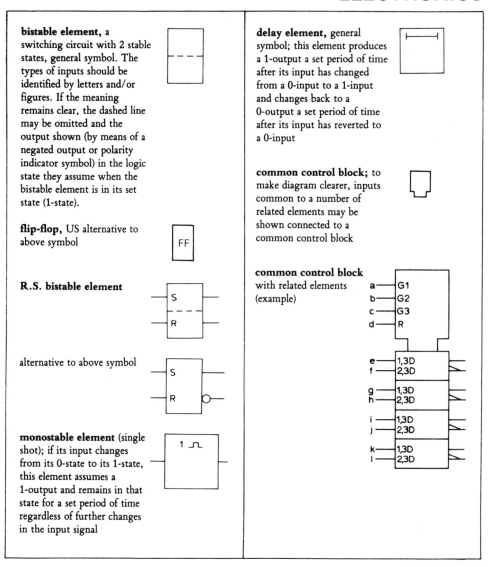

bistable element, a switching circuit with 2 stable states, general symbol. The types of inputs should be identified by letters and/or figures. If the meaning remains clear, the dashed line may be omitted and the output shown (by means of a negated output or polarity indicator symbol) in the logic state they assume when the bistable element is in its set state (1-state).

flip-flop, US alternative to above symbol

FF

R.S. bistable element

S
R

alternative to above symbol

S
R

monostable element (single shot); if its input changes from its 0-state to its 1-state, this element assumes a 1-output and remains in that state for a set period of time regardless of further changes in the input signal

1 ⊓

delay element, general symbol; this element produces a 1-output a set period of time after its input has changed from a 0-input to a 1-input and changes back to a 0-output a set period of time after its input has reverted to a 0-input

common control block; to make diagram clearer, inputs common to a number of related elements may be shown connected to a common control block

common control block with related elements (example)

a	G1
b	G2
c	G3
d	R
e	1,3D
f	2,3D
g	1,3D
h	2,3D
i	1,3D
j	2,3D
k	1,3D
l	2,3D

The following symbols and conventions are used in conjunction with the draughting conventions and symbols for materials and building elements given under *Architecture*. They are in common use but variations to them will be found as there is no universally accepted standard. Other sections relevant to civil and structural engineering are *Geology* and *Mathematics*.

STRUCTURAL GRID CONVENTIONS

Structural grids are frequently used on plans of buildings with reasonably regular structures in order to provide a reference for structural members and their location. They also provide a convenient means of describing the location of general constructional components and details.

The lines of the grid follow the lines of the structure; normally through the centres of the beams and columns. The grid, therefore, need not necessarily be rectalinear of dimensionally uniform. Generally the grid lines are denoted by numbers (1, 2, 3, etc) in one direction and by letters (A, B, C, etc) in the other; either commencing at the top lefthand corner of the drawing (as recommended in *Standard Method of Detailing Reinforced Concrete* — The Concrete Society and The Institution of Structural Engineers) or at the bottom lefthand corner of the drawing (recommended by BS publications, *CI/Sfb Project Manual* — Alan Ray-Jones and Wilfred McCann, RIBA Services Ltd and others). A column can then be denoted by the references of the grid lines passing through its centre, and a beam by the references of the grid line at one end, its centre line and the grid line at the other end. Floor slabs and large openings in the structure can be denoted by the references of grid lines forming their boundaries.

The location of the structural grid in relation at the site boundaries is normally ascertained and given on the found floor plan or the site plan and, in larger scale projects especially, the relationship of the structural grid to the national cartographic grid (in Britain — the National Grid) can be also given.

grid (example)

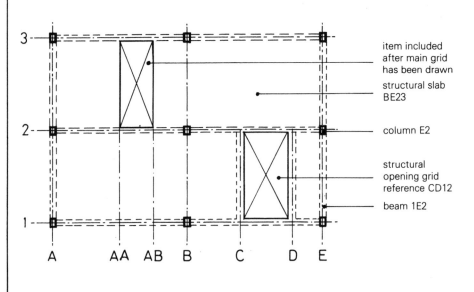

item included after main grid has been drawn

structural slab BE23

column E2

structural opening grid reference CD12

beam 1E2

alternative structural grid
(example), used especially to describe steel structures. References to vertical members are indicated by being encircled and may be marked 'S' (for 'stanchion'). Beam references consist of the reference number of the stanchion directly below or to the left (on plan) plus an even number, if horizontal, or an odd number, if vertical (on plan).

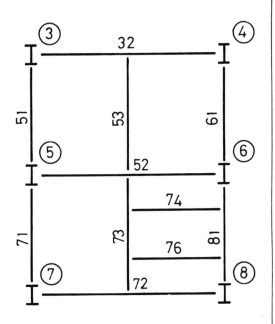

eccentricity of stanchion in relation to grid and beam in relation to centre of stanchion at each end, on plan (example)

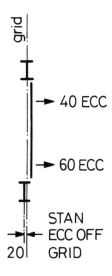

ENGINEERING 1

CONVENTIONS FOR DETAILING CONCRETE REINFORCEMENT

In accordance with the *Standard Method of Detailing Reinforced Concrete* (see *Structural Grid Conventions* above)

bar reinforcement symbol (on plan) (example) — the long thick line indicates the length and location of one bar; the other bars being located as that bar but off-set at the stated centres between its location and the bar location indicated by the short thick line. The reference notation gives information in the following sequence: the number of bars, type, size, bar mark number, bar centres in mm, location or comment. The notation '8Y16 — 3 — 200T' = 8 high yield high bond bars of 16mm diameter, bar mark 3, at 200mm centres in the top of the slab.

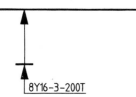

8Y16–3–200T

The preferred sizes of metric round bars(in mm)are 8, 10, 12, 16, 20, 25, 32, 40.

The following abbreviations may be used with this system of notation:

R	round mild steel bars
Y	high yield high bound strength bars
X	other types not covered by R or Y
EF	each face
FF	**far face**
NF	near face
B	bottom
T	top
EW	each way

staggered reinforcement (example); where bars are to be located in a staggered fashion, the arrangement is indicated by two or more thick lines (representing bars) — with the implication that the given arrangement should be repeated the appropriate number of times.

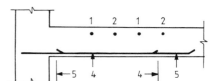

5Y16–5–200T

bar reinforcement in elevation and section (example showing bars in elevation in bottom and in section in top of a slab), bars are referenced by their bar mark only.

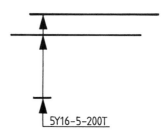

reinforcing fabric in bottom of concrete slab

reinforcing fabric in top of concrete slab

reference mark (example) of the reinforcing fabric, which should be written along the diagonal. Where there might be any doubt as to the direction of the main wires, a **double-headed arrow** should be drawn across the diagonal to indicate the direction.

US CONVENTIONS FOR DETAILING CONCRETE REINFORCEMENT

Note: In general, the conventions used in the USA for detailing concrete reinforcement are different from those given above; also, metric measurements are not used.

bar reference notation gives information in the following sequence: number of bars, size, type bend, length, spacing, location. For instance, in the notation 20-8A 41-6 @ 12, TF ('20' specifies the number of bars, '8' specifies the size ½ inch round, 'A' specifies the type band — straight for this example, 41-6 specifies the length, '12' designates the spacing, and 'TF' designates the location as top face). 'BF' implies bottom face.

reinforcing fabric should be drawn (ie not shown by the conventions given in the previous section) with the size given, and the orientation of wiring and spacing described if they are not the same in both directions.

HOLES — and structural openings

structural opening, ie large opening through structure

large hole

large hole

small hole

small hole

hole; requires written identification

Note: The size of holes (ie width and length, or diameter) should be given with the above conventions.

METAL SECTIONS

'I' section $\mathbf{I}$

angle — equal sided (legs) L

angle — unequal (legs) L

tee section T

channel section C

'C' section C

'Z' section Z

bulb angle

bulb plate

Note: In the US, the following nomenclature, recommended by the AISC (American Institute of Steel Construction), is normally used for the above sections:

W	wide flange beam(s)
M	light weight beam(s)
S	I-beam(s)
L	angle(s) — designated 'equal (or) unequal leg angles L'

ENGINEERING 1

WT wide flange structural tee(s) cut from rolled beam(s) **MT** light weight structural tee(s) cut from rolled beam(s) **C** American standard channel section(s)	**MC** miscellaneous channel section(s) 'C' and 'Z' sections, bulb plates and bulb angles are usually designated by a written description.

Except where stated otherwise, the following symbols conform with BS 1553: Part 1: 1977. Where marked IHVE they are derived from the IHVE Guide Part C published (1970) by the Institution of Heating and Ventilation Engineers (now known as the Chartered Institute of Building Services). Where possible, alternatives to the following symbols are given in the following German (DIN/ISO) and USA sections.

PIPES and connections and flow direction indicators

pipe, general symbol (the thicker the line the greater the flow rate)

concealed pipe

future pipe

pipe at high level (IHVE) or **existing pipe**

pipe in roof or above ceiling (heating or ventilation plans only)

crossing pipes, not connected

pipe connection (tee)

direction of flow

direction of rise (IHVE)

Note: BS 1553: Part 1 recommends an arrow parallel to the pipe annotated with the word 'fall' or 'rise' and a ratio indicating the rate of fall or rise.

flexible hose (flanged example)

existing pipe to be removed

land drain mole (BS 1192)

land drain tile (BS 1192)

drain (outside building), general (BS 1192)

pipe perpendicular to plane of drawing

pipe, heated or cooled (heating or cooling medium to be annotated adjacent to symbol)

jacketed pipe (heating or cooling medium to be annotated adjacent to symbol)

lagged pipe

sleeved pipe (fluid or fill of the annulus to be annotated adjacent to symbol)

PIPE JOINTS

spigot and socket

flanged joint (IHVE) or **flanged and bolted**

compression joint

expansion joint

butt welded

soldered or solvent welded

screwed

sleeve (BS 534)

socket welded (BS 3799)

swivel

ENGINEERING 2

electrically bonded

electrically insulated

union joint (IHVE)

VALVES

valve (in line), general symbol

angle valve (simple screw-down)

three-way and four-way valves are indicated by additional outlet sections as appropriate, eg three-way valve

non-return valve

safety (relief) valve

pressure reducing valve (IHVE)

butterfly valve

globe valve

ball valve

wedge gate valve

parallel side valve

needle valve

diaphragm valve

plug valve

flanged valve

OTHER PIPEWORK FITTINGS AND EQUIPMENT

end cap, general symbol (annotated as 'detachable' when appropriate)

end cap, butt-welded

end cap, screwed

end cap, fillet-welded

end screwed and plugged

end closure — quick release

end socket and spigot

guide (support)

indication of support points

anchor, general symbol	
Note: BS 1553 includes a number of variations to the above symbol for use as alternatives should specific support and hanger symbols be necessary.	
hydrant	
sprinkler head (BS 1192)	
gully (BS 1192)	
intercepting trap (a grease trap can be indicated by substitution of the abbreviation GT or IT) (BS 1192)	
trap release or retention	
filter or strainer	
radiator	
spray device	
manhole, surface water (BS 1192)	
manhole, foul water (BS 1192)	
pump (IHVE)	
rotary pump, fan or simple compressor	
open vent	
exhaust head	

bursting disc	

DUCTS and flow direction indicators

duct (first figure, dimension of side shown; second figure, dimension of side not shown)	350×210
duct, concealed	
two-dimensional representation	
duct at high level on plan or in front of section	
two-dimensional representation	
duct in false ceiling (for plans only)	
two-dimensional representation	
direction of flow, outlet or exhaust	
direction of flow, inlet or supply	
change in size only	
rectangular or oval to round	
change in shape or size, single line convention	
bend in (rectangular) duct, section visible	
two-dimensional representation	

ENGINEERING 2

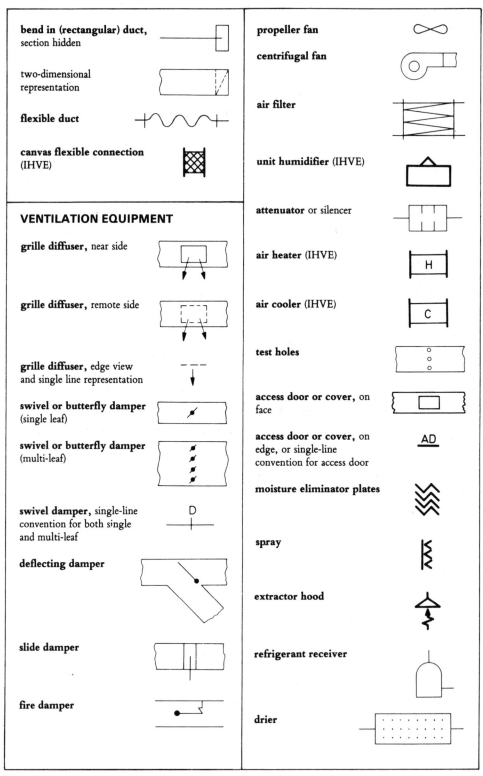

bend in (rectangular) duct, section hidden

two-dimensional representation

flexible duct

canvas flexible connection (IHVE)

VENTILATION EQUIPMENT

grille diffuser, near side

grille diffuser, remote side

grille diffuser, edge view and single line representation

swivel or butterfly damper (single leaf)

swivel or butterfly damper (multi-leaf)

swivel damper, single-line convention for both single and multi-leaf

deflecting damper

slide damper

fire damper

propeller fan

centrifugal fan

air filter

unit humidifier (IHVE)

attenuator or silencer

air heater (IHVE)

air cooler (IHVE)

test holes

access door or cover, on face

access door or cover, on edge, or single-line convention for access door

moisture eliminator plates

spray

extractor hood

refrigerant receiver

drier

CONTROL AND MONITORING COMPONENTS
for both plumbing and ductwork

Note: These symbols are used in conjunction with other pipework and ductwork symbols (especially valve symbols) as appropriate; eg

manual screw-down valve

manual isolation

spring

weight loaded

float control

piston

diaphragm

motor

power signal

solenoid

statically loaded

quick opening

quick closing

dash pot checked

meter, any type (the letter 'F' indicates flow measurement)

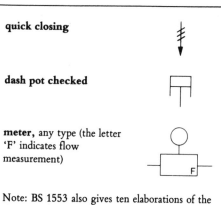

Note: BS 1553 also gives ten elaborations of the above meter symbol, each indicating a specific method of metering, ie turbine, diaphragm, etc.

manual actuating element

automatic actuating element with integral manual actuating element

automatic actuating element or point of measurement

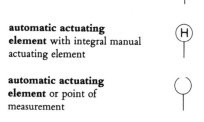

Note: A system for further defining the above symbol for an automatic actuating element is set out in ISO 3511/1 (BS 1646: Part 1: 'Symbolic Representation for Process, Measurement Control Functions and Instrumentation'). This includes a one, two or three letter code for use within the above symbol with meanings as follows:

As first letter (measured or initiating variable)

D density
E all electrical variations (should be further defined)
F flow rate
G gauging, position or length
H hand (manually initiated) operated
K time or time programme
L level
M moisture or humidity
P pressure or vacuum
Q quality
R nuclear radiation
S speed
T temperature
U multi-variable
V viscosity
W weight or force

ENGINEERING 2

As second letter (qualifies first letter)
D difference
F ratio
J scan
Q integrate or totalize
R recording

As second or third letter (action)
A alarm
C controlling
I indicating (need not be used with self-indicating recorders)
Q integrating or summating
S switching
T transmitting
Z emergency or safety acting

ABBREVIATIONS

commonly used with plumbing and ductwork graphic symbols

AD access door

B brine (IHVE)
BFW boiler feed water (IHVE)

C condensate (IHVE)/cooker, domestic (BS 1192)
CA compressed air (IHVE)
CF cold feed (IHVE)
CHW chilled water (IHVE)
CLW cold water service (IHVE)

D damper/drain (IHVE)/dry (IHVE)
DP discharge soil pipe (BS 1192)

F fuel (IHVE)/flow (IHVE)
FA from above (IHVE)
F & E feed and expansion (IHVE)
FB from below (IHVE)
FD fire damper
FS foul sewer (BS 1192)

G gas in domestic installations (BS 1192)/gulley (BS 1192)

GT grease trap (BS 1192)

H hand/hydrant (BS 1635)/heater (IHVE)
H/C heater-cooler
HL high level (IHVE)
HPHW high pressure hot water (IHVE)
HWS hot water, domestic (IHVE)

IT intercepting trap (BS 1192)

LL low level (IHVE)
LPHW low pressure hot water (IHVE)

M motor
MH manhole (BS 1192)
MPHW medium pressure hot water (IHVE)
MWS mains water (IHVE)

OV open vent (IHVE)

P pressure (IHVE)

R refrigerator, domestic (BS 1192)/refrigerant (IHVE)/return (IHVE)
RE roddng eye (BS 1192)
RWO rainwater pipe (BS 1192)
RWS rainwater shoe (BS 1192)

S steam (IHVE)/sprinkler (BS 1192)/sink (BS 1192)
SD sliding damper
SW surface water drain (BS 1192)
SWS surface water sewer (BS 1192)

T temperature (IHVE)
TA to above (IHVE)
TB to below (IHVE)
TW treated water (IHVE)

V vent (IHVE)/vacuum (IHVE)
VP vent pipe (BS 1192)

W wet (BS 1635, IHVE)
WD washbasin (BS 1192)
WH water heater, domestic (BS 1192)
WM washing machine, domestic (BS 1192)

Except where stated otherwise, the pipe, pipe joint, valve and other pipework fitting and equipment symbols and the abbreviations conform with ANSI Z32.2.3: 1949 (r1953) and the duct, ventilation equipment, refrigeration/cooling equipment and control and monitoring component symbols conform with ANSI Z32.2.4: 1949 (r1953). These were adopted as American national standards in 1969. Where possible, alternatives to the following symbols are given in the adjacent German and British sections.

PIPES

cold water

drinking water flow

drinking water return

hot water

hot water return

soil, waste or leader above grade

soil, waste or leader below grade

vent

pneumatic tube runs

branch and head (sprinkler system)

drain (sprinkler system)

main supplies (sprinkler system)

Note: ANSI Z32.2.3 gives further broken lines and dot-dash symbols for identifying pipelines in drawings of air-conditioning systems and heating systems. A number of these symbols are visually similar to the above symbols.

In addition to graphic symbols, other pipes and pipe contents are identified by abbreviations given in breaks in the line-forms delineating the pipe routes (see *Abbreviations* below); eg

compressed air

PIPE CONNECTION FITTINGS
including elbow, base and crossover fittings

Note: The following fittings are shown with screw joints. Alternative symbols can be formed by substituting bell and spigot, flanged, welded or soldered joint symbols for the screw joint symbol (see *Pipe Joints* below); eg

flanged tee

straight cross

reducing cross (example)

double branch

side outlet (outlet down)

side outlet (outlet up)

tee

tee (outlet down)

tee (outlet up)

tee (double sweep)

tee (single sweep)

ENGINEERING 3

crossover		**bushing** (screwed)	
elbow 90°		**bushing** (welded)	
elbow (turned down)		**bushing** (soldered)	
elbow (turned up)		**expansion joint** (bell and spigot)	
base		**expansion joint** (flanged)	
long radius		**expansion joint** (screwed)	
		expansion joint (weleded)	
reducing radius (example)		**expansion joint** (soldered)	

PIPE JOINTS
including expansion joints and bushing

bell and spigot	
flanged	
screwed	
welded	
soldered	
union (flanged)	
union (screwed)	
union (welded)	
union (soldered)	
bushing (bell and spigot)	

VALVES
Note: The following symbols are all shown with screwed joints unless stated otherwise.

gate valve, also used for general stop valve when amplified by specification	
gate valve angle (elevation)	
gate valve angle (plan)	
check valve straight way	
check valve angle	
check valve straight way, bell and spigot	
safety valve	
reducing pressure valve (ANSI Z32.2.4)	
relief valve (ANSI Z32.2.4)	

reducing valve, automatic (flanged)

by-pass valve, automatic (flanged)

governor-operated valve (flanged)

globe valve

globe valve angle (plan)

globe valve angle (elevation)

diaphragm valve

cock

float valve

motor-operated valve

angle hose valve

gate hose valve

lockshield valve

quick-opening valve

float valve, high side (ANSI Z32.2.4)

float valve, low side (ANSI Z32.2.4)

OTHER PIPEWORK FITTINGS AND EQUIPMENT

cap (screwed)

cap (bell and spigot)

bull plug (flanged)

bull plug (bell and spigot)

pipe plug (screwed)

pipe plug (bell and spigot)

anchor (ANSI Z32.2.4)

hanger or support (ANSI Z32.2.4)

vent point

air eliminator (ANSI Z32.2.4)

pump, type (eg vacuum) should be indicated (ANSI Z32.2.4)

heat transfer surface, plan view, type (eg convector) should be indicated (ANSI Z32.2.4)

thermostatic trap (ANSI Z32.2.4)

blast thermostatic trap (ANSI Z32.2.4)

ENGINEERING 3

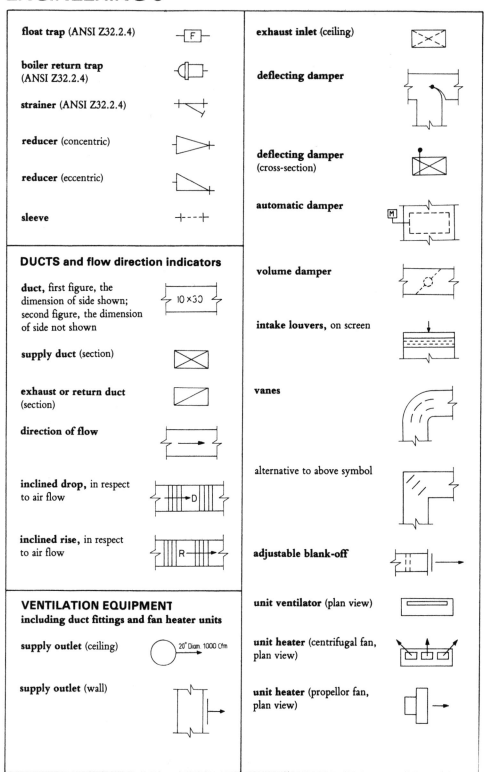

float trap (ANSI Z32.2.4)

boiler return trap
(ANSI Z32.2.4)

strainer (ANSI Z32.2.4)

reducer (concentric)

reducer (eccentric)

sleeve

DUCTS and flow direction indicators

duct, first figure, the
dimension of side shown;
second figure, the dimension
of side not shown

10 × 30

supply duct (section)

exhaust or return duct
(section)

direction of flow

inclined drop, in respect
to air flow

inclined rise, in respect
to air flow

VENTILATION EQUIPMENT
including duct fittings and fan heater units

supply outlet (ceiling)

20" Diam. 1000 Cfm

supply outlet (wall)

exhaust inlet (ceiling)

deflecting damper

deflecting damper
(cross-section)

automatic damper

volume damper

intake louvers, on screen

vanes

alternative to above symbol

adjustable blank-off

unit ventilator (plan view)

unit heater (centrifugal fan,
plan view)

unit heater (propellor fan,
plan view)

REFRIGERATION, COOLING EQUIPMENT AND COMPONENTS

fan or forced air, used as component of other symbols

filter and strainer

compressor

compressor with open crankcase, reciprocating, belted

compressor with open crankcase, reciprocating, direct drive

compressor with enclosed crankcase, rotary, belted

condenser, air cooled, finned, static

condenser, water-cooled, concentric tube in a tube

condensing unit (water-cooled)

condensing unit (air-cooled)

drier

cooling tower

evaporator, manifolded, gravity air, finned

evaporator, plate coils headered or manifold

finned type cooling unit, natural convection

forced convection cooling unit

scale trap

thermal bulb

immersion cooling unit

heat exchanger

CONTROL AND MONITORING COMPONENTS

Note: These symbols are used with other pipe or ductwork symbols as appropriate.

pressurestat

pressure switch

thermostat

thermostat (remote bulb)

gauge

ABBREVIATIONS
commonly used with plumbing and ductwork and graphic symbols

A	compressed air
ACID	acid waste
AD	access door (ANSI Z32.2.4)

B	brine		**L**	louver (ANSI Z32.2.4)
BR	brine return		**LR**	long radius
C	condenser water flow		**M**	motor (ANSI Z32.2.4)
CH	circulating chilled or hot water flow (in air conditioning drawings)		**P**	pressure (ANSI Z32.2.4)
CHR	circulating chilled or hot water return (in air conditioning drawings)		**PA**	anchor
CR	condenser water return		**R**	relief (ANSI Z32.2.4)/rise, ie inclined rise in respect to air flow (ANSI Z32.2.4)/return
CS	compressor suction (ANSI Z32.2.4)		**RS**	refrigerant discharge
D	drop ie inclined drop in respect to air flow (ANSI Z32.2.4)		**RL**	refrigerant liquid
			RS	refrigerant suction
E	exhaust duct (ANSI Z32.2.4)		**S**	supply duct (ANSI Z32.2.4)/snap action (evaporator pressure regulating valve) (ANSI Z32. 2.4)/sprinkler (mains supplies or drain)
F	fire line pipe/float ((ANSI Z32.2.4)			
FOF	fuel oil flow			
FOR	fuel oil return			
FOV	fuel oil tank vent		**T**	thermostat (ANSI Z32.2.4)
G	gas		**V**	vacuum cleaning pipeline
H	hanger (ANSI Z32.2.4)/humidification line			

The following symbols conform with the ISO draft proposals which have been adopted as a standard by DIN (ref DIN ISO 4067:Part 1). See the preceding sections for the British and the US alternatives.

PIPES and connections and flow direction indicators

pipe, general symbol

pipe, visible at section

pipe, concealed at section

pipe, in front or above section

Note: The standard also gives a range of broken and dot-dash line forms to be used as an alternative to the above symbols, should it be desirable to differentiate between various fluids carried by pipes. The standard does not specify which particular fluid is to be indicated by each given line form.

crossing pipes, not connected

pipe connection (tee)

direction of flow

direction of fall

flexible pipe (hose)

PIPE JOINTS

joint, general symbol

spigot and socket

flange

collar

expansion joint

VALVES

valve, general symbol; also two-way valve

three-way and four-way valves are indicated by additional outlet portions as appropriate; eg three-way valve

non-return valve (flow direction is from the non-solid to the solid part of the symbol)

safety valve

reducing valve

OTHER PIPEWORK FITTINGS AND EQUIPMENT

cap nut

sliding support

anchor point

air purging device

vacuum breaker

ENGINEERING 4

draw-off point		**DUCTS and flow direction indicator**
		duct, general symbol
hydrant, general symbol		
sprinkler head		**supply duct,** visible section
gully, general symbol		
gully, with trap		
separator, general symbol		
steam trap		**supply duct,** hidden section
filter		
heater		
mixing tap		
shower		**exhaust duct,** visible section
trap, views		
trap, in section		
drain and inspection cover		
pump		**exhaust duct,** hidden section
apparatus, general symbol. (It is preferred that the circular symbol be used for apparatus in which there are rotating parts, and the rectangular symbol for any other apparatus.)		
		direction of flow

ENGINEERING 4

VENTILATION EQUIPMENT

apparatus, general symbol.
As *Other Pipework Fittings and Equipment* above

air supply fitting

air exhaust fitting

damper

air grille

fan

air filter

humidifier

silencer

air heater

air cooler

CONTROL AND MONITORING COMPONENTS

Note: These symbols are used in conjunction with other pipework and ductwork symbols as appropriate; eg

hand-operated valve

hand-operated, general symbol

automatic, general symbol

spring

weight

float

piston

diaphragm

electric motor

solenoid

temperature sensing

pressure sensing

flow sensing

humidity sensing

level sensing	Note: The indicating gauge and recorder symbols can be used with the various sensing symbols to identify different types of indicating and recording instruments; eg
indicating gauge or meter	**pressure gauge** (located on pipe)
recorder	

The symbols given in this section are a selection of those commonly used by academic and commerical geologists and engineers throughout the world. However, there is no universally agreed range of geological mapping symbols — most geological surveys and even certain companies having their own variations. Common variations have been included below. Those marked (USGS) conform with the symbols given in the *List of Geologic Map Symbols* (1977) published by the United States Geological Survey. Those marked (BMR) conform with a standard range of geological symbols compiled by the staff of the Australian Bureau of Mineral Resources.

The symbols are used to record observations and measurements made in the field onto (generally) large-scale field maps, and also in the collating of geological information onto various types and scales of maps and diagrams. These maps and diagrams may be used for communication or record purposes, or as an aid to solving structural and stratification problems.

The principal elements shown are the location of geological features and the measurement and location of strike, dip and plunge of geological features. (In field maps the location of collected samples may also be of great importance.) In geology, strike is the direction in which a horizontal line could be drawn over a surface of a geological feature. Orientation of strike is conventionally given in degrees east (or clockwise) of north. Dip is the slope of a surface of a geological feature at 90° from the strike; ie the maximum angle of slope. Measurement of dip is given in degrees from the horizontal. Plunge is the angle a fold axis or other geological line makes with the horizontal. Measurements and notation of strike, dip and plunge are indications of the geological form of a landscape.

A geological fault is a fracture in rock where there is an observable displacement of the rock masses on either side of the fracture. A normal fault is an inclined fracture where the rock strata above the fault plane have been displaced downwards in relation to the strata below. In a reverse fault the strata above the fault plane have been displaced relatively upwards. A thrust fault is a near-horizontal dislocation where the rock beneath the fault plane appears to have acted as a wedge thrusting the rock above upwards. An anticline is an upward fold or arch of strata, while a syncline is a downward fold or trough of strata.

Patterns for indicating zones of different rocks are used more frequently on geological sections than on geological maps where they may obscure other map detail. Colour tints are often employed to indicate rock types on maps as they tend to obscure other detail less. However, no range of colour tints is included here because of the lack of common ground between the various standard ranges in existence.

Topographic symbols (see *Cartography*), hydrogeological symbols (see *Hydrogeology*), mining plan symbols (see *Mining*) and oil and gas well symbols (see *Petroleum*) may all be used in conjunction with the following geological symbols.

GEOLOGY

CONTACTS

or boundaries between rock units or geological formations

contact — position accurate (USGS, BMR) or observed

contact — approximate or uncertain (USGS, BMR),

A broken line is used where a boundary extends or may extend beyond the width of the drawn line. In general a longer-dash line is used to imply an uncertain or assumed location and a shorter-dash line is used to imply a lesser degree of uncertainty. USGS proposes a short-dash line should imply any definite contact (including gradational contacts, inferred contacts, and indefinite boundaries of superficial deposits).

inferred contact, alternative to above symbol for inferred contacts only (BMR)

concealed contact, projected beneath mapped units (USGS, BMR)

inferred, concealed contact (BMR)

contact showing dip, arrow in direction of dip, barbs may be omitted (USGS)

contact showing dip, alternative to above symbol

unconformity (break in the normal succession of older to younger strata), observed, tops of 'v's or 'u's face younger rocks (BMR)

unconformity, used in sections only (BMR)

facies boundary, generally schematic only (BMR)

FAULTS

fault — position accurate (USGS, BMR) or **fault — observed**

fault — position approximate (USGS, BMR)

fault — existence uncertain (USGS) or **fault — inferred** (BMR)

concealed fault (USGS, BMR)

concealed fault — existence uncertain (USGS) or **concealed fault — inferred** (BMR)

vertical fault (BMR); if marked 90° conforms with USGS

low-angle thrust fault, 'T' on upper plate (USGS, BMR)

thrust or reverse fault, saw-teeth on upper plate (USGS) or **normal fault,** teeth on downthrown side (BMR)

thrust fault, teeth on upper plate, alternative to above symbol

high-angle reverse fault, teeth on downthrown side (BMR)

normal fault, hachures on downthrown side, used on special tectonic maps (USGS, BMR)

direction of movement of block, used in conjunction with above fault symbols

fault showing **relative horizontal movement** (tear fault, wrench fault or transcurrent fault) (USGS, BMR)

fault showing **bearing and plunge of relative movement of block,** may be used with normal fault or high-angle reverse fault symbol to conform with BMR

20

fault showing **dip and lineation**

50 60

Note: The following abbreviations may be used with the above fault symbol:

b   breccia (in fault)
m   mylonite (in fault)
q   quartz-filled fault
U   upthrown side
D   downthrown side

quartz-filled fault, example of above

q   q

fault zone, showing dip

25

fault zone, showing dip (BMR)

30

shear zone (USGS)

shear zone (BMR)

fault breccia (BMR, USGS)

FOLDS

anticline crestal plane (USGS) or crest (BMR), if this symbol is used primarily for the axial plane of anticlines — then a crest line may be indicated by the same symbol with the words 'showing crest line'

anticline — position approximate (BMR) or **inferred or probable articline** (USGS); the line may be interspersed with question marks to imply 'doubtful' (USGS) or 'inferred' (BMR)

anticline — concealed, the line may be interspersed with question marks as with symbol above (USGS, BMR)

asymetrical anticline crestal plane; short arrow indicates steeper limb (USGS)

syncline trough plane (USGS) or trough (BMR), line may be solid, dashed, dotted, or interspersed with question marks as with the symbols for anticline above. If symbol is used for axial plane, trough may be indicated by same symbol with the words 'showing position of trough'.

axis; 'f' added to above anticline or syncline symbols when axis rather than crest or trough is mapped (BMR)

f

monocline (USGS, BMR)

plunge arrow, added where necessary to above anticline and syncline symbols, (example giving angle of plunge) (USGS)

35

dip of axial plane (example giving angle of dip); dip indicator may be used with the above anticline or syncline symbols

60

overturned anticline (USGS, BMR)

GEOLOGY

overturned syncline, (USGS, BMR)

bearing and plunge of axis of overturned anticline (example giving angle of plunge); bearing and plunge can be similarly indicated on above overturned syncline symbol (BMR)

plunge of **minor anticline** (USGS, BMR)

plunge of **minor syncline** (USGS, BMR)

plunge of **drag fold** (BMR)

plunge of **fold axes** where beds are too tightly folded to show individual folds (USGS, BMR)

plunge of **minor folds** showing 'S', 'Z' and 'M' vergences (BMR)

anticline

syncline

anticline, used on tectonic maps (BMR)

anticline — concealed, used on tectonic maps (BMR)

syncline, used on tectonic maps (BMR)

syncline — concealed, used on tectonic maps (BMR)

BEDDING — strike and dip of beds or strata

strike, dip not determined (BMR)

strike and dip, example giving measured angle of dip (USGS, BMR)

srike and dip uncertain

combined symbol example, dip and strike of bedding and trend and plunge of lineation

strike of vertical beds, may be marked 90° to conform with BMR

horizontal beds (BMR)

horizontal beds (USGS)

strike and dip of **overturned beds,** example giving measured angle of dip (USGS, BMR)

proved direction of facing, based on sedimentary structures, indicated by dot (BMR examples — 'strike and dip of strata' and 'strike and dip of overturned strata')

prevailing dip of gently folded beds (BMR)

prevailing dip of strongly deformed beds (BMR)

generalized strike and dip of crumpled or undulating beds (USGS, BMR)

curving dip, example giving maximum and minimum angles (BMR)

dip slope, observed, arrow as long as exposed slope (BMR)

top of bed, arrow shows facing, base at point of observation (BMR)

facing of lava-flow top, base of arrow at point of observation (BMR)

FOLIATION AND CLEAVAGE
ie mineral banding and parallel lines of fracture in rock

strike and dip of foliation, example giving measured angle of dip (USGS, BMR)

Note: The above symbol is sometimes used for all forms of foliation, cleavage and schistosity, or, alternatively, for the strike and dip of bedding.

strike of **vertical foliation** (USGS, BMR)

horizontal foliation (USGS, BMR)

strike of foliation, dip not determined (BMR)

strike and dip of cleavage (USGS, BMR)

strike of **vertical cleavage** (USGS, BMR)

horizontal cleavage (USGS, BMR)

strike of cleavage, dip indeterminable (BMR)

additional symbols used to distinguish various types of planar structures

LINEATIONS
ie one dimensional features in rock or rock surface including alignment of minerals, flow lines, inclusions and streakings

bearing of **lineation — general** (USGS), or bearing of **lineation — mineral elongation** (BMR)

bearing of **lineation — general** (BMR)

bearing of **lineation — bedding-cleavage intersection** (BMR)

bearing of **lineation — crenulation** (BMR)

combined symbol, example giving strike and dip of foliation and plunge of lineation (USGS, BMR)

combined symbol, example giving strike and dip of foliation and rake (lineation measured in plane of foliation) (BMR)

vertical lineation (USGS, BMR)

horizontal lineation (USGS) or **horizontal lineation — mineral elongation** (BMR)

JOINTS

strike and dip of joint, example giving measured degree of dip (USGS)

strike and dip of joint, example giving measured degree of dip (BMR)

strike of vertical joints (USGS)

strike of vertical joints (BMR)

horizontal jointing (USGS, BMR)

GEOLOGY

MINERAL DEPOSITS — dykes, veins and outcrops

vein or dyke (BMR)

vein (USGS)

stringers or veinlets of ore (USGS)

dyke (USGS)

altered wall rock, showing intensity of alteration by concentration of dots (USGS)

ore body (USGS) or **mineral outcrop** (BMR)

Note: The above six symbols may be drawn in red or another colour to differentiate types and grades.

minor mineral occurrence; example shows copper (BMR)

·Cu

unworked deposit; example shows salt (BMR)

PATTERNS for indicating rock types
Note: The following are indications of the traditional use of commonly-found patterns only. Weight and spacing of line and stipple, and the particular meanings attached to specific versions of each pattern, vary greatly.

sand, standstone, quartzite, arkose, etc

Note: Dots combined with other rock symbols normally indicate sandy forms of these rocks.

argillaceous rocks, ie clay, shale, siltstone, claystone, slate, etc

sandy argillaceous rocks (sandy clays, shale, etc)

pebbles, boulders, conglomerate

sandy conglomerate, pebbly sandstone, etc

limestone, dolomite, chalk

tuff or tuffaceous sandstone

breccia, tuff and/or agglomerate

sandy limestone

chert or flint layers (marks may be hatched or shaded rather than solid black)

igneous and volcanic rocks; note that 'V's are frequently incorporated into patterns indicating rocks of volcanic origin — see *tuff* below.

coal

OTHER SYMBOLS
including glacial striae, fossil, volcanic, thermal and location of section

glacial striae (or small grooves produced as a result of ice movement); ice movement direction uncertain (BMR)

glacial striae; arrow indicates direction of ice movement which produced grooves

fossil locality (BMR)

alternative to above symbol

alternative to above symbol

macrofossil locality (BMR)

microfossil locality (BMR)

GEOLOGY

plant fossil locality (BMR)

fossil wood (BMR)

vertebrate fossil locality (BMR)

Note: The abbreviations 'm' (**marine**), 'b' (**brackish water**) and 'f' (**freshwater**) may be used with the above fossil symbols. Also these symbols may be bracketed to indicate sparse occurrence or underlined to indicate abundance.

vent, general symbol, should be coloured (BMR); may be used with the following abbreviations:

NR no topographic relief
V vent (used where symbol may be confused with symbol for bore or oil well)

Other abbreviations to imply chemical or petrological characteristics.

major eruptive centre (crater or vent) with recorded eruption (BMR)

major eruptive centre (crater or vent) with no recorded eruption (BMR)

subsidiary eruptive centre with recorded eruption (BMR)

subsidiary eruptive centre with no recorded eruption (BMR)

crater or caldera wall (BMR)

Note: 'H' may be used with other volcanic symbols in this section to imply thermal activity.

lava flow, true outline should be shown (BMR)

type section, short (BMR)

type section, long (BMR)

Note: In the above two symbols, the arrow points mark ends of section.

geological section (BMR)   A ├──────┤ B

102

This section gives the Greek letters in their normal alphabetical order. The English rendering of each letter's name has been provided; followed by (in brackets) the nearest English equivalent of the letter as it is believed to have been pronounced in Ancient Greek; followed by the capital and then the lower-case forms of the letter. Modern Greek employs the same alphabet but many of the letters are pronounced in a markedly different manner.

The sign 'ς' is used only when sigma is the last letter of a word; eg αἰσθητικος (aesthetic). 'H' originally stood for an 'h' sound but came to be used to indicate a long 'e'. The presence of an 'h' sound before a vowel (ie an aspirated vowel) is indicated by the 'rough breathing' symbol placed before a capital vowel or over a lower-case vowel; eg ἱππος = hippos (horse). Unaspirated vowels are indicated in a similar manner by the 'smooth breathing' symbol.

See other sections, such as *Mathematics, Astronomy* and *Units of Measurement,* for the use of Greek letters to signify meanings in addition to the names and phonetic sounds given below.

alpha (a)	A	*a* or α	**mu** (m)	M	μ
beta (b)	B	β	**nu** (n)	N	ν
gamma (g)	Γ	γ	**xi** (x)	Ξ or Ζ̃	ξ
delta (d)	Δ	δ	**omicron** or **omikron** (short o)	O	o
epsilon (short e)	E	ε	**pi** (p)	Π	π
zeta (z)	Z	ζ	**rho** (rh)	P	ρ
eta (long e)	H	η	**sigma** (s)	Σ or C	σ
theta (th)	Θ	θ	**tau** (t)	T	τ
iota (i)	I	ι	**upsilon** (u)	Υ	υ
kappa (k)	K	κ	**phi** (phi)	Φ	φ or φ
lambda or **labda** (l)	Λ	λ	**chi** (ch)	X	χ

GREEK ALPHABET

psi (ps)	Ψ ψ	**smooth breathing** '
omega (long o)	Ω ω	Note: In words ending in a long vowel followed by '*ι*', the '*ι*' is written as a small letter under the vowel (ie as a *iota subscript*) – unless the word is written in capitals. Iota subscripts are also used elsewhere in a few words; eg ιδια (privately), ωου (egg).
rough breathing	'	

Heraldry is one of many systems employing geometric and pictorial devices as identity emblems which have been used throughout the world since early times. However, few of these, except perhaps the Japanese Mon system, reached the level of complexity and social significance of traditional European heraldry.

In Europe, heraldry developed in the Middle Ages primarily as a means of identifying individuals by symbols both on their armour worn in battle and at tournament, and on the personal seals needed to 'sign' documents, at a time when few people could read or write. Heraldic symbolism was applied to many aspects of a knight's armour and equipment, but the shield provided the prime surface on which to display an identification symbol and has remained the one essential element in any traditional armorial achievement or 'coat of arms'.

Until the end of the Middle Ages anyone, except a serf, was free to assume arms, and many sections of society did assume arms because of their usefulness as seals and trademarks. From the year 1400 onwards, kings began to grant arms and, in certain countries, heralds were charged with issuing and recording these grants — hence the term 'heraldry'. Heralds had been employed since the twelfth century for a number of duties, such as the supervision of tournaments and funerals, and to act as emissaries, all of which required a good knowledge of heraldic devices. In Britain, arms continue to be granted on behalf of the Crown by the Kings of Arms (the most senior heraldic officers) at the College of Arms (the heraldic office for England, Wales and Northern Ireland), and the Lord Lyon. The Lord Lyon has the power to fine or imprison at the Court of the Lord Lyon (the heraldic office for Scotland). The Chief Herald of Ireland in Dublin is responsible for heraldry in Eire.

In most other European countries, anyone is free to assume arms, although some governments require certain arms to be registered. Outside Europe, many people of European descent continue to bear their ancestral arms and many new arms and emblems have been adopted — many of which portray local fauna and flora. People of British descent may be granted or confirmed arms through the heraldic offices in the British Isles and the post of Chronicler King of Arms in Spain still exists to register the right to Spanish Arms. Because of heraldry's association with the aristocracy, when the aristocracy has been overthrown (as during the French and Russian revolutions), traditional heraldry has tended to be rejected and new forms of emblems adopted.

Family arms are inherited in much the same way as names. Under the feudal system in western Europe, a title could be held by one person at a time and so the practice developed of 'differencing' family arms by adding a charge (a device applied onto a shield) called a 'cadency mark' or by altering them in some other way, so that no two men carried the same arms. A system of differencing, chiefly by the use of different bordures, is continued in Scotland and, to a lesser extent, differencing by cadency marks, as a matter of courtesy, is continued in England and Ireland.

In English-speaking countries, a heraldic description of arms is referred to as a 'blazon' and special heraldic terminology is used which is largely derived from Norman French — the language of the English nobility in feudal times. Unfortunately this terminology is not international, many countries employing a different terminology; for instance,

HERALDRY

'ordinaries' are called *pièces honorables* in French and *Heroldstücke* or *Heroldsbilder* in German.

The principal sources for the information given in this section are the works of Carl-Alexander bon Volborth.

PARTS OF AN ACHIEVEMENT OF ARMS

Note: A complete heraldic device, ie a shield with or without helmet, crest, motto and so forth, which many people refer to as a 'coat of arms', is more properly called an 'achievement'. A 'coat of arms' more correctly refers to a linen coat carrying an individual's heraldic device that was sometimes worn over a suit of armour, or to the same device applied to a shield.

1 **shield**
2 **helm (helmet)**
3 **mantling**
4 **crest**
5 **torse (crest-wreath)**
6 **supporters**
7 **motto**
8 **compartment**
9 **cri-de-guerre** (war-cry) or
    slogan (in Scotland)
10 **banner**
11 **manteau (robe of estate)**
12 **crown, coronet of rank**

Note: An achievement rarely contains all of the above items. Usually an individual's achievement contains no more than a shield, helmet, mantling, torse, crest and motto.

SHIELD FORMS

Note: A great variety of shapes have been used for armorial shields; particularly elaborate versions being fashionable in the sixteenth, seventeenth and eighteenth centuries after shields, no longer used in battle, became completely obsolete when tournaments fell from favour after the death of Emperor Maximillian I in 1519.

heater shaped

with **rounded base**

lozenge shape; used for the arms of women — mainly in western Europe and Italy

oval; sometimes used by married women — especially in the Netherlands. In Napoleonic heraldry, arms for women consisted of an oval shield between two palm branches

shields with a notch for a lance are called **à bouche**

horse-head shield; used particularly in Italy since the Renaissance; possibly developed from an armoured plate worn on the face of a knight's horse

PRINCIPAL POINTS OF THE SHIELD

Note: Arms are described from the view point of the bearer of the arms — hence dexter (right) and sinister (left) appear reversed.

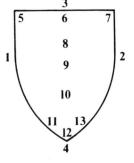

1	**dexter side**
2	**sinister side**
3	**chief**
4	**base**
5	**dexter chief**
6	**middle chief**
7	**sinister chief**
8	**honour point**
9	**fess point**
10	**nombril**
11	**dexter base**
12	**middle base**
13	**sinister base**

COLOURS AND METALS

Note: The following are the traditional colours used in heraldry. The patterns shown below or the actual colours may be used. The patterns enable arms to be engraved. In Britain, three other traditional colours (some called 'stains') also may be used; tenne (tawny), sanguine (a shade of red) and murrey (mulberry). Other colours may be included in the natural representation of items — naturally coloured items are described as 'proper'. The term 'tincture' is applied to mean colour, metal or fur. Normally a colour should not be superimposed on a colour or a metal on a metal.

argent, silver (white)

or, gold (yellow)

sable (black)

gules (red)

azure (blue)

HERALDRY

vert (green)

purpure (purple)

FURS

ermine

ermines

erminois

Note: The above three stylised versions of ermine are more common in heraldry in Britain than in the rest of Europe where ermine is more frequently depicted in its natural form in trimmings and linings of items other than the sheild.

vair, a pattern of blue and white representing the back and belly fur of the squirrel. Note, if this pattern is in any other colour, the fur is described as 'vairy'. In Germanic countries, a 'vairy' pattern consisting of two colours and two metals is called 'Buntfeh'.

counter-vair

vair en point

potent

counter-potent

natural fur; frequently used in the arms of furriers and furrier guilds

PRINCIPAL DIVISIONS OF THE SHIELD

per fess

per pale

per bend

per bend sinister

per chevron

quarterly or per cross

counter-quartered

per saltire

gyronny of eight

per pall or tierced in pairle

tierced in fess; a shield may also be tierced in pale (divided into three vertically), tierced in bend, or tierced in bend sinister

Note: The above divisions may be combined to produce further sub-divisions of sections of a shield, as in the following example, or the dividing lines between parts of a sheild may not be straight but varied as in *Ornamental Edges* below.

per pale, the sinister half per fess

HERALDRY

ORDINARIES AND SUBORDINARIES

Note: Ordinaries and subordinaries are traditional, easily-distinguishable devices on a sheild. They may be indicated in various tinctures and their edges varied from straight lines (as indicated in *Ornamental Edges* below). Although opinions vary as to what constitutes ordinaries and subordinaries, the chief, pale, bend, fess, chevron, cross and saltire are generally considered ordinaries.

chief

fess

bars

barry (implies an even number of six or more stripes)

barrulets

fess cotised

pale. Note a number of vertical bars may be called 'paly' or 'pallets'.

paly (implies an even number of six or more stripes)

pallets (pallets must divide the shield into an odd number of five or more sections)

pale cotised

chevron. Note a number of chevrons together are referred to as 'chevronels'.

cross

baton

saltire

billet

bend

pile

bend sinister

pall

Note: The incorporation of a bend sinister or bendlet sinister into the father's arms was a widely used method of *differencing the arms of illegitimate children* in early heraldry. However, many other methods were also employed; for instance, some would carry their father's arms on a chevron, bend or fess on an otherwise undecorated sheild or use their father's arms with a diferent bordure.

canton

inescutcheon

bendlets

bordure	**fretty**
orle	three **annulets** or rings
double tressure	Note: The following six subordinaries may also be referred to simply as roundels of a particular tincture.
flanches	three **torteau** (gules). The most famous use of torteau is in the arms of the Medici family (originally six torteau on a gold background, in 1465 Piero de Medici was granted the right to replace one torteau with a roundel containing the arms of France).
gyron	three **hurts** (azure)
fret	three **pomeis** (vert); singular — pomme

three **bezants** (or); a field covered in gold roundels may be described as 'bezanty'

three **pellets** (sable)

three **plates**

lozenge; a field covered in lozenges may be described as 'lozengy'

mascle

fusil

label of three points; may be used as a cadency mark (see below)

Note: Groups of annulets, torteau, fusils, billets, etc may be arranged in fess (across the centre of a shield), in chief (across the top), in pale (vertically down the centre), in bend (diagonally across a shield), in chevron (in the form of a chevron), etc.

ORNAMENTAL EDGES

engrailed

bend engrailed

invected

bend invected

arched or **enarched**

double arched

nowy

HERALDRY

wavy or **undy**		**dovetailed**	
alternative to above symbol		**potenty**	
nebuly		**urdy**	
alternative to above symbol			
radiant or **rayonny**			

THE CROSS

Note: Being a religious symbol and the emblem of the crusaders, the cross has been one of the most widely used and important heraldic devices. It appears in many different styles and decorative forms.

indented		**latin cross**	
dancetty			
dancetty floretty			
bevilled		arms of the Order of the **Knights Templar** (Militia Christi); founded in 1118 and abolished by Pope Clement V in 1312	
angled		arms of the **Teutonic Order** (Orden der Ritter des Hospitals St Marien des Deutschen Hauses zu Jerusalem); founded in 1190, converted to a religious order of chivalry in 1190 and changed to a clerical order with priests and lay brothers and sisters (Bruder des Deutschen Ordens St Mariens zu Jerusalem) in 1928	
escartelly			
embattled			
battled, embattled or **embattled grady**			
raguly		**Greek cross**	

arms of **Switzerland** (couped white cross on a red background); earliest known use is as a military banner in Bern in the thirteenth century

cross botony

St Andrew's cross; used as the device on the flag of Scotland

cross fleuretty

cross of Lorraine or patriarchal cross

cross flory

Tau cross or cross of St Anthony

cross moline; used as cadency mark on the arms of an eighth son (in English heraldry)

cross of Malta; the Sovereign Military Order of Malta was formally recognized by the papacy in 1113. After the loss of the Holy Land, the order moved to Rhodes, then Malta. The knights were also called the Knights of St John (after St John the Baptist — patron saint of their original hospital in Jerusalem).

cross formy fitchy

arms of **Neukölln;** a West Berlin *Land* which belonged to the Order of St John from 1312 to 1435

cross crosslet

insignia of **St John's Ambulance Brigade** (Britain)

cross formy

HERALDRY

cross pommy

cross potent

cross counter-quartered

HERALDIC CREATURES

Note: The following are traditional, mainly unnatural, creatures found represented in heraldry, and consist largely of stylised early attempts to depict unseen real and mythical beings. Many naturally represented animals are also used as heraldic devices — especially in modern heraldry.

heraldic **tiger** or **tyger**; a naturalistic tiger is described as a 'Bengal tiger'.

Note: A **mantygre** is similar to the above device but is drawn with the face of bearded man with two straight horns on his forehead.

heraldic **panther**

lion rampant; a widely used device; the Royal Arms of Scotland consist of a 'lion rampant within a double tressure flory counter-flory gules'

the arms of **Norway** with lion rampant clutching an axe (symbol of St Olav)

the arms of **Czechoslovakia** (Adopted 1960): the lion device on a red field is drvied from the old arms of Bohemia.

lion passant guardant, sometimes referred to as a **leopard;** three lions passant guardant were used in the arms of the king of England from the twelfth century onwards

the arms of Denmark: containing three **lions passant** (the arms originated in the twelfth century)

Note: Lions may be used in many other attitudes including 'sejant' (seated), 'conchant' (crouched), 'statant reguardant' (standing, looking towards tail), 'dormant' (sleeping) and 'sejant affronty' (seated facing forwards).

winged lion with halo; symbol of St Mark and used in the city arms of Venice

Agnus Dei (Lamb of God), Paschal Lamb

winged bull with halo; symbol of St Luke

heraldic **pelican vulning its breast**; in mediaeval times, the pelican was believed to wound its breast to feed its young with its own blood — so became a Christian symbol for self-sacrifice. If standing on its nest feeding its young, the pelican is described as being 'in its piety'.

martlet; used as the cadency mark of a fourth son in English heraldry

eagle.

The emperors of the Holy Roman Empire (962-1806) adopted the eagle as their device (probably as a reference to the imperial eagle — see below). The double-headed eagle (see below) was a device of the Byzantine or Eastern Roman Empire which ended in 1453 when the Turks conquered Constantinople (Byzantium). From about 1400, the Holy Roman emperors generally used the double-headed eagle, while the single-headed eagle remained the emblem of the German king before being crowned emperor. The double-headed eagle continued to be used by the Austrian Empire (1804-1919) after the end of the Holy Roman Empire. A single-headed eagle was adopted as the German imperial emblem when Germany was united in 1871. Thus single and double-headed eagles (normally black) may be found in the arms of many people and places with connections with the above empires — not just in Austria and Germany but also in Savoy, Switzerland, northern Italy, the Balkans, Hungary, Bohemia, Poland and the Netherlands.

doubled-headed eagle;

the imperial emblem of the Byzantine, Holy Roman and Austrian empires (see *eagle* above), also adopted as a device by Ivan III of Russia (1462-1505) who, married to Sophia (niece of the last Byzantine ruler), considered himself heir to the Byzantine Empire. Hence the use of the double-headed eagle in the arms of Imperial Russia.

HERALDRY

arms of the canton of **Geneva;** composed of the Key of St Peter (the patron saint of the city cathedral) and an eagle

arms of the **United States** of America (adopted in 1782). The Bald Eagle (native to N. America) is shown in its natural colours.

arms of the **Republic of Austria;** the broken fetters were added after the liberation from Nazi Germany in 1945

arms of **Mexico** (adopted 1823); the device is derived from Aztec mythology

arms of the **Federal Republic of Germany**

phoenix;

eagle with halo (symbol of St John the Apostle and the badge of Aragon) supporting the arms of the **kingdom of Spain**

mythical bird that after living five or six hundred years in the Arabian desert, burns itself on its funeral pyre and rises renewed from its own ashes — hence symbolizes rebirth or rebuilding after destruction (particularly by fire)

imperial eagle (eagle with a thunderbolt);

female **griffin;** half lion and half eagle with eagle's wings. If 'rampant', as shown, the griffin is described as 'segreant'.

the symbol of Jupitor as used on the standards of the ancient Roman Legions. This symbol was directly adopted by Napoleon I as his imperial arms on becoming Emperor of France (1804) and was subsequently used by Napoleon III. Napoleonic sovereign princes were permitted a golden eagle on the chief of their shields.

male **griffin;** resembles a female griffin but without wings

opinicus; seen in English Heraldry only

salamander, (in heraldry) a mythical reptile that lives in fire; hence symbolizes the spirit of fire or immunity to fire

Chinese dragon; a golden dragon was the symbol of the Chinese imperial family

dragon segreant

(red) **dragon passant** as it appears on the badge of Wales

lindwurm, a German traditional dragon-type monster; half-dragon/half-serpent — often without wings

wyvern, sometimes known as a 'basilisk' although this term may refer to a form of wyvern with a dragon's head at the end of its tail

cockatrice

heraldic **dolphin;**

a dolphin has been in the arms of the French royal heir apparent, the Dauphin (dolphin), since 1349 when the last of the Dauphins of Viennois bequeathed his lands to the French king with the condition that the eldest royal son should thenceforth bear the Dauphins' title and arms.

fish naiant;

(if vertical with head down — 'fish urinant', if vertical with head up — 'fish hauriant'). Fish appear in the arms of guilds of fishermen, fishmongers and seamen.

heraldic **sea-lion;** normally has webbed feet in English heraldry

heraldic **sea-horse;** normally has webbed feet in English heraldry

HERALDRY

unicorn; a symbol of virginity and purity

heraldic **ibex** or antelope

yale; seen in English heraldry only

Pegasus; a winged horse of Greek myth; winged horses are used sometimes in modern heraldry to symbolize air transport or speed

centaur; in Greek myth, a member of a tribe of horse-people living in the mountains of Thessaly. **Sagittarius** is symbolized by centaur shooting with a bow and arrow.

chimera; a female monster originally a mixture of lion, goat and serpent (according to Homer) but which, in heraldry, may also be shown as various combinations of those creatures, the head and breasts of a woman, a dragon's tail and, in certain cases, wings

mermaid or **siren;** often shown holding a mirror and combing her hair

merman or **triton;** normally shown holding either a trident (as right) or blowing a murex (shell)

double-tailed mermaid or **melusine**

harpy, a rapacious monster or, in Norse myth, one of the beings which carried off the souls of warriors killed in battle to feast at Valhalla

Greek **sphinx;** in Greek mythology, a monster who sat on a rock in Thebes, killing all Thebans when they failed to answer the riddle she asked – until Oedipus answered the riddle and she killed herself by jumping off the rock

Egyptian **sphinx;** should have a man's or an animal's head but usually drawn with a woman's head and breast

HERALDIC PLANTS AND FLOWERS

fleur-de-lis, a symbol of the Holy Virgin; best known use is in the arms of the French monarchy. Also used as the cadency mark of a sixth son in English heraldry.

the **Tudor rose;** the red rose badge of Lancaster and the white rose badge of York were combined to form the Tudor badge by Henry VII of England

the **Luther rose,** the emblem of Martin Luther

Note: A rose is the cadency mark of a seventh son in English heraldry.

thistle, the floral badge of Scotland

shamrock, the badge of Ireland

emblem of the **Emperor of Japan**

OTHER CHARGES
including cadency marks

label, the cadency mark of an eldest son during his father's lifetime — in English, Scottish, and Irish heraldry

crescent, the cadency mark of a second son — in English heraldry

molet or mullet (from *molette,* spur-rowel), the cadency mark of a third son — in English heraldry

annulet, the cadency mark of a fifth son — in English heraldry

octofoil or double quatrefoil, the cadency mark of a ninth son — in English heraldry

Note: See above for the English cadency marks of a fourth son (a martlet), a sixth son (a fleur-de-lis), a seventh son (a rose), and an eighth son (a cross moline).

decrescent

increscent

the **Keys of St Peter**; with the papal tiara (see below), these form the insignia of the papacy

cross staff (example), part of a bishop's insignia of office

crosier (example), part of a bishop's insignia of office

Note: In Catholic heraldry, according to an instruction given by Pope Paul VI in 1969, crosiers and mitres (see below) should not be used except by a diocese which may display a mitre with cross and crosier, and an abbey which may display a mitre with crosier.

portcullis, the badge of the Beauforts — used by the Tudors to display their Beaufort descent

the **rod of Aesculapius,** a symbol of the medical profession

Note: Pestles and mortars and covered cups were symbols of apothecaries.

the **caduceus** or rod of Mercury; used as a symbol for trade and commerce

horn of plenty or cornucopia

hammer, a symbol for industry or the industrial workers — best known as used combined with sickle symbol (see below) in the emblems of communist parties and the USSR. Also see the arms of the Republic of Austria above.

sickle, a symbol of agriculture or the agricultural workers — best known as used combined with the hammer symbol (see above)

Note: Tradesmen and guilds of tradesmen have frequently used the tools of their trade and/or their products as emblems, eg *scissors* (tailors), *barrels* (brewers), *axes* or *bulls' heads* (butchers), *tongs* and *hammers* (blacksmiths). *Ships* and *anchors* are frequently used in the arms of places and individuals connected with seafaring.

HELMS, CROWNS AND OTHER HEADWEAR

Note: Helms (helmets) are not normally shown on the arms of women. Royal helms are usually all gold and drawn facing front. Generally the amount of gold or gilding shown on the helm decreases in accordance with the social rank of the individual. In British heraldry, peers' helms are shown in profile, in silver with the opening guarded by gold bars; baronets' and knights' helms are steel, possibly with garnishings of gold, and facing front with open vizor; lower ranks' helms are all steel and in profile with closed vizors.

great helm or barrel helm

tilting helm or frog-mouthed helm; used in jousting (the head was tilted forward during the charge to enable the wearer to see and then raised just before impact to avoid the danger of the opponent's lance piercing the eye-piece)

armet or vizored helm (with vizor closed); became a popular form of tournament helm in the sixteenth century. In France and Belgium, a golden armet with vizor open, facing front, became the helm for the arms of a king.

barred helm

the **crown of St Stephen;** very much a national, historic emblem of Hungary — the actual crown disappeared in World War II

Note: Royal arms usually display crowns resembling those actually worn by the monarchy. Lesser ranks — barons, counts and so on — display lesser crowns (coronets).

Italian **mural crown;** mural crowns are frequently displayed in city arms

cap of the Doge of Venice; used as a crest by families descended from a doge

chapeau or cap of maintenance; associated with armorial bearings of peers (in England) or feudal barons (in Scotland)

HERALDRY

Phrygian cap (Phrygia — an ancient country in Asia Minor), a symbol of liberty; used much during French revolution and also featured in various South American arms

bishop's mitre (example); used in the arms of bishops and archbishops. No longer in general use in the Catholic church — see *crosiers* above.

the **tiara,** the papal crown which with the Keys of St Peter (see above) form the insignia of the Pope

arms of a **cardinal** (example — the arms of Francis, Cardinal Spellman, Archbishop of New York) showing the standard insignia of the red cardinal's hat with 15 tassels on either side

Note: The arms of other Catholic ecclesiastical ranks may display similar hats but in different colours and with varying numbers of tassels; eg a *patriarch* — green hat with 15 tassels on either side, an *archbishop* — green hat with ten tassels on each side, a *bishop* — green hat with six tassels on each side, an *abbot and provost* — black hat with six tassels on either side, a *priest* — black hat with one tassel on either side.

deacon's hat;

in the Church of England, clergymen of ranks below bishops (who use mitres) may use in their arms a black deacon's hat with the colour and number of tassels as prescribed to his office in place of a helm and crest. Deacons use the hat as above – without tassels.

The international traffic signs proposed in discussions at the United Nations after the Second World War have been generally adopted by European countries. Except where stated otherwise, the following road signs and markings conform to those given in *European rules concerning road traffic signs and signals,* published by the European Conference of Ministers of Transport. The ECMT constitutes a forum for the ministers of transport from 19 countries; viz Austria, Belgium, Denmark, Finland, France, Germany, Greece, Ireland, Italy, Luxembourg, the Netherlands, Norway, Portugal, Spain, Sweden, Switzerland, Turkey, the United Kingdom and Yugoslavia, and with the associated countries of Australia and Japan.

The conventions agreed by members of the ECMT allow for certain degree of variation between the signs adopted by different countries and for individual countries to adopt additional signs within the framework of the agreed conventions to meet particular needs. Hence there are certain local minor differences in the form of different signs; for example, the pedestrian silhouette symbol may or may not have a hat. More importantly, in countries where traffic keeps to the left, such as the United Kingdom, many signs are a mirror-image of those shown below. This difference applied not only to signs displaying traffic movements by arrows and so forth but also to signs warning of potential dangers such as animals which are shown emerging from the left of the road — ie the most dangerous quarter for a driver keeping to the left. Where it has been thought useful, signs which are peculiar to the United Kingdom have been included.

All the member countries of the ECMT employ the following conventions for traffic light signals;

Non-flashing lights

green light	vehicles may proceed if the way or junction is clear
amber light	vehicles must stop at the 'stop line' (see below) or traffic light — unless they are so close to the junction or signal when the amber light appears that it would be dangerous to do so
red light	vehicles must stop at the 'stop line' or before the traffic light if there is no 'stop line' (but never on the junction)
amber and red light together	vehicles must stop and remain stopped although the signal is about to change
green illuminated arrow	vehicles may go in the direction indicated by arrow despite any other signal light showing

Flashing lights

red flashing light	or a signal formed of two red lights flashing alternately stop at the 'stop line' or before the signal if there is no 'stop line' (this system is frequently used at railway level crossings) or (if used above a lane of a motorway) proceed no further in this lane
amber flashing light	or a signal formed of two amber lights flashing alternately proceed but with particular care

ROAD MARKINGS

Note: Road markings should be white or near white (ie shades of silver or light grey) except for markings showing where parking is permitted which may be blue or markings showing where parking is prohibited which may be yellow. (Blue lines are not used as above in UK.)

lane line (along the road)

centre line (along the road)

warning line (used along the road before a dangerous section; particularly before a section where it is dangerous to overtake)

single continuous line (along the road) — vehicles must not cross or straddle this line. (Generally not used in UK except as in note below.)

Note: Where necessary, similar lines to the above may also be applied along roads to mark clearly the edge of the carriageway.

double line (along the road) — alternative to the above marking

continuous and broken lines (along the road) — vehicles may cross these lines (ie to overtake) and return to their correct lane if the broken line is the line nearest their lane and it is safe to do so

a **stop line** across one or more traffic lanes marks the position behind which drivers must stop at a junction or traffic light

UK alternative (being phased out) for the above marking

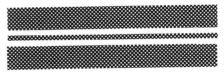

a **give-way line** across one or more traffic lanes marks the position at junctions behind which drivers must give way or allow priority to traffic using the road beyond the line

UK alternative to the above marking

give-way warning mark may be applied to the road surface on the approach to a give-way line (see above)

a **cyclist crossing** should be marked by broken lines of squares or parallelograms

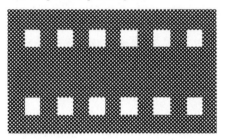

a **pedestrian crossing** should be marked by broad stripes parallel to the axis of the carriageway

Note: Alternatives to the above markings do exist; in particular for those pedestrian crossings regulated by lights (known as 'pelican' crossings in UK).

parking is prohibited where a zig-zag line is applied along the edge of a carriageway (this convention not used in the UK) or where the road is marked as described in the following note

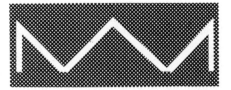

Note: Parking is also prohibited or subject to regulations stated by other means where there is a continuous or broken yellow line along the kerb or edge of the carriageway. A continuous line also implies that vehicle standing or waiting is similarly prohibited or restricted. In Britain, a single yellow line indicates no waiting during at least eight hours between 7 am and 7 pm for four or more days each week (ie normally during the working day); a double yellow line indicates the same restrictions as single yellow line plus some additional restricted period after 7 pm; a broken yellow line implies that waiting is limited and/or prohibited at certain times of the day or some other lesser restriction than that indicated by continuous lines.

restricted loading or unloading (in UK) is indicated by yellow marks on the kerb at right angles to the roadway together with white plates with written details of the restrictions. Individual yellow marks imply a minimum level of restriction, pairs of yellow marks indicate no loading or unloading for at least eight hours between 7 am and 7 pm for four or more days each week, while groups of three yellow marks indicate the same as pairs of marks plus some additional restriction after 7 pm or, alternatively, no loading or unloading at any time.

HIGHWAY SIGNS 1

JUNCTION AND PRIORITY SIGNS

Note: See *Warning Signs* below for signs at level crossings and at the approach to junctions. See introductory note for the significance of light signals.

give way at intersection (white or yellow with red border); not used in the UK at intersection, but used with a distance plate to give advance warning of stop or give-way requirements (see *give-way line* in *Road Markings* above)

UK version of the above sign as used at an intersection (white with red border — words 'GIVE WAY' in black)

stop at the 'stop line' (see *Road Markings* above) (white on red ground)

earlier version of above sign (red on white ground — word 'STOP' in black)

priority road; used to notify users of a road that, at intersections of that road with other roads, the drivers of vehicles moving along those other roads should give way to them (yellow, black and white) (not used in UK)

end of priority; road ceases to have priority over other roads (colours as above sign with black diagonal bar) (not used in UK)

priority for oncoming traffic; used on narrow sections of road; positions of arrows reversed if traffic keeps to the left (black and red on white or yellow ground)

priority over oncoming traffic; used on narrow sections of road; positions of arrows reversed if traffic keeps to the left (red and white on blue ground)

PROHIBITORY SIGNS and signs ending prohibitions or restrictions

Note: These prohibitory signs consist of black symbol(s) on a white or yellow background surrounded by a red circular border, unless stated otherwise. Any oblique bars across a prohibitory sign should be red.

no entry (white on red disk)

closed to all vehicles in both directions

no entry for any power-driven vehicles except two-wheeled motor cycles without side cars

no entry for motor cycles

no entry for cycles

no entry for power-driven agricultural vehicles (not used in UK)

no entry for mopeds (not used in UK)

no entry for vehicles with over 12 seats except regular scheduled school and works services (UK sign)

no entry for goods vehicle

Note: A tonnage figure may be added to 'no entry' signs to indicate that vehicles are only prohibited if above that weight.

no entry for vehicles carrying more than a certain quantity of explosives or readily inflammable substances (black and orange symbol on white ground with red border)

no entry for power-driven vehicles drawing a trailer other than a semi-trailer or single-axle trailer (not used in UK)

no entry for vehicles carrying more than a certain quantity of substance liable to cause water pollution (orange, black and blue symbol on white ground with red border)

no entry for pedestrians

Note: No entry for combinations of classes of traffic may be indicated by groups of the above signs or the silhouettes of the prohibited types of traffic included together on the same sign: eg

no entry for power-driven vehicles

no entry for animal-drawn vehicles

UK version of the above sign

no entry for handcarts (not used in UK)

no entry for vehicles wider than the specified number of metres or feet (example)

no entry for vehicles or combinations of vehicles longer than the specified number of metres or feet (example)

no entry for vehicles higher than the specified number of metres or feet (example)

no entry for vehicles or vehicles and load heavier than the specified number of tonnes (example)

no entry for vehicles or vehicles and load weighing more than the specified number of tonnes on any one axle (example)

driving of vehicles less than the specified distance apart is prohibited (not used in UK)

no left turn

no right turn

no U-turns (note the 'U' is reversed to accord with traffic movement where traffic keeps to the left)

no overtaking (the locations of the red and black car silhouettes are reversed in countries where traffic keeps to left) (red and black symbols on white ground with red border)

no overtaking by goods vehicles, ie goods vehicles with a permissible maximum weight over 3.5 tonnes (red and black symbols on white ground with red border) (not used in UK)

speed limit; maximum permitted speed is specified (example)

no sounding of horns or other audible warning devices (not used in UK)

customs — passing without stopping prohibited (the sign should contain the word 'customs' in two languages)

Note: Variations of the above sign may be used to indicate 'no passing without stopping' for other reasons — which should be given in a brief written form instead of the word 'customs'.

end of local prohibition or restriction imposed on vehicles. The sign may consist of black or grey diagonal band (or a diagonal band consisting of black or grey parallel lines) on a white or yellow ground. National regulations continue to apply. (In UK, this sign with a black band on white implies that the national speed limit applies.)

ending of a specified prohibition (example — end of speed limit of 40 kph or mph); as sign above but includes the symbol for the particular prohibition which has ended (in light grey) (not used in UK)

parking prohibited; the scope of the prohibition may be detailed on a plate below this sign (red diagonal on blue ground with red border). In the UK the roundel usually appears on a small yellow rectangular sign which also includes details of the scope of the restriction.

no stopping or 'clearway' (red diagonals on blue disk with red border)

alternative parking; parking is prohibited on odd-number dates (white numeral and red diagonal on blue disk with red border) (not used in UK)

alternative parking; parking is prohibited on even-number dates (colours as above sign) (not used in UK)

Note: The above two signs need not imply the changeover time is midnight. If domestic legislation prescribes an alternation other than a daily one, the numerals I and II should be replaced by that period of alternation, eg 1-15 and 16-31 for an alternation on the 1st and the 16th day of each month.

MANDATORY SIGNS and lane control signs

Note: These mandatory signs are circular with white (or near white) symbols on a blue background, unless stated otherwise.

direction to be followed; examples indicate 'straight ahead', 'left', 'right', 'straight ahead or right'. The sign indicating 'straight ahead or right' is not used in the UK.

pass this side, ie side indicated by arrow (example)

compulsory **roundabout** (where traffic keeps to the left, the direction of the arrows is reversed). In the UK, this symbol is used for a 'mini-roundabout'.

cycle track to be used by no other motor vehicles except mopeds if so required by domestic legislation or indicated by an additional sign with an inscription or the silhouette of a moped

footpath to be used only by pedestrians

bridle-path not to be used by road-users except for those on horseback

minimum speed (example shows a minimum speed of 30 kph or mph)

end of minimum speed requirement (example) (colours as above sign but with a red diagonal)

snow chains compulsory on not less than two of any vehicle's driving wheels (black and white symbol on blue ground) (not used in UK)

lane control signals used over a road; the white, downward-pointing arrow means that the lane below is available and the red cross means that the lane below is closed to traffic facing the signal. The background to the symbols is normally black. (UK sign)

MOTORWAY SIGNALS

Note: These signals consist of black ground on which symbols are illuminated together with amber or red flashing lights (see introductory note). The signals are switched on when conditions on the motorway are abnormal: those mounted on the central reservation or behind the hard shoulder apply to all on-coming traffic; those mounted above the roadway are applicable to the individual lane beneath. The versions of these signals given here are as used in the UK.

temporary maximum speed

lane closed ahead

change lane

leave motorway at the next exit

end of restriction (ie road clear)

WARNING SIGNS

Note: These signs giving warning of danger ahead consist of a black symbol on a white or yellow equilateral triangle with a red border, unless stated otherwise.

left bend

right bend

double bend or succession of bends, the first to the right

double bend or succession of bends, the first to the left

steep descent (example) — the figure gives the gradient as a percentage

steep ascent (example) — the figure gives the gradient as a percentage

dual carriageway ends (UK sign)

carriageway narrows, general symbol

carriageway narrows from left

Note: In the UK, the above two signs may have a plate below them reading 'Single file traffic' (ie single file in each direction) or 'Single track road' (ie road only enough for traffic in one direction at any time).

swing bridge

quay or river bank

dips, ridges, hump bridges or **road in bad condition,** general symbol

HIGHWAY SIGNS 1

ridge or **hump bridge** (this sign is to be used in the UK to indicate a speed control hump)

British sign for **hump bridge**

dip (not used in UK)

slippery road

loose gravel or **chippings**

danger from **falling rocks** or **fallen rocks**

height limit given in feet and inches, or metres (example), eg low bridges (UK sign). UK bridges that are not so signed are normally 16½ feet high in the centre of the road.

tunnel (UK sign)

pedestrian crossing ahead

children (eg exit from school or playground)

pedestrians in road ahead (UK sign)

crossing point for **elderly people** or **handicapped**; used with plate stating 'Elderly', 'Blind' or 'Disabled' people (UK sign)

cyclists; a similar sign used in the UK to indicate 'cycle route ahead' has the cycle symbol without the rider

domestic animals (sign should be a silhouette of the form of animal most frequently encountered)

wild animals (sign should be a silhouette of the form of animal most frequently encountered)

overhead electric cable; used with plate giving maximum safe height for vehicles beneath (UK sign)

road works

UK verion of above sign

traffic signals (traffic lights); three alternatives corresponding to different arrangements of lights (red, amber, green symbol on white ground with red border)

traffic signals; UK version of above signs (colours as above sign but with black surround to red, amber and green disks)

failure of traffic signals (UK sign) (red, amber and green disks and red diagonal on black ground with white border)

low flying **aircraft**

prevailing strong **cross winds**

two-way traffic (arrows reversed where traffic keeps to the left)

two-way traffic across one-way carriageway ((UK sign)

intersection where the priority is that prescribed by the general priority rule in force in the country (not used in UK)

intersection with a road the users of which must give way (5 alternatives corresponding to specific forms of intersection)

T junction (UK sign)

traffic merging with equal priority from right (UK sign)

traffic merging with equal priority from left (UK sign)

change to opposite carriageway ahead; may be reversed (UK sign)

sharp deviation of route to left — or right if chevrons are reversed (white chevrons on black ground); in UK version ground is red if deviation is temporary

temporary lane or road closure (UK sign)

roundabout (arrows reversed if traffic keeps to the left)

level crossing with gates or staggered half-gates

level crossing other than with gates as above

intersection with **tramway line** ahead (not used in UK)

level crossing; sign used at crossing (white or yellow ground, red or black border)

alternative to above sign for crossings with more than one track (white or yellow and red or black)

additional signs used to give warnings on the **approach to level crossing** (red bars on white ground)

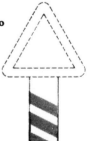

danger(s) other than those indicated by other signs; the nature of the danger may be written on a plate beneath the sign

INFORMATIVE SIGNS

Note: These signs are usually rectangular (although direction signs may be in the shape of an elongated rectangle terminating in an arrowhead) with white or light-coloured symbols on a dark field or dark-coloured symbols on a white or light-coloured field. Red should be used rarely for these signs and should never predominate.

advance direction signs (examples)

no through road advance direction sign (example) (red and white on blue ground)

no through road sign placed at entry to road (red and white on blue ground)

advance direction sign (example showing route to be followed in order to turn left where a left turn at the next intersection is prohibited)

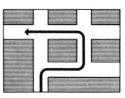

choice of direction in different lanes prior to a junction (example)

direction of a place (examples)

direction of an **airfield** (example)

direction of a **camping-site** (example)

direction of a **youth hostel** (example)

beginning of a built-up area (example) (not used in UK)

end of a built-up area
(example) (not used in UK)

Note: In the UK, direction signs are normally white on a blue background on motorways, white and yellow on a green background on primary routes and black on white on lesser traffic routes. Temporary directions are normally given by signs in black on a yellow ground.

pedestrian crossing;

the panel should be blue or black, the triangle white or yellow and the pedestrian symbol black or dark blue (not used in UK)

hospital,

drivers should take precautions near medical establishment, eg not make unnecessary noise (white on blue ground)

alternative to above symbol

(red cross and white symbol on blue ground) (not used in UK)

sign confirming direction of **one-way road** (white on blue)

UK version of above sign (white on blue)

alternative to above **one-way road** sign; placed approximately parallel to road and may be marked 'one-way' in language of location (white on blue) (not used in UK)

distance markers;

indicating the distance to the start of a deceleration lane on a motorway (white on blue) or on a primary route (white on green) or on a non-primary route (black on white); each bar represents 100 yds (UK sign)

motorway;

sign placed at point where special rules to be observed on a motorway begin to apply (white on blue). In UK, sign includes motorway's reference number, eg M25.

Note: A warning of the approach to a motorway may be given by the above sign with an inscription giving the distance to the motorway or with a sign attached resembling the following example.

distance to dangerous section or to the beginning of zone to which a regulation or regulations apply (example); supplementary sign with the distance written in black or dark blue on a white or yellow field with a black, dark blue or red rim or written in white or yellow on a black or dark blue field with a white, yellow or red rim.

end of road for motor vehicles only.

This sign may also be used to give warning of the end if containing an inscription giving the distance to the end of such a section of road (red diagonal on white symbol on blue ground) (not used in UK).

end of motorway.

This sign may also be used to give warning of the end of a motorway; it should then include an inscription giving the distance to the end (white on blue with red diagonal)

bus stop (not used in UK)

road for motor vehicles only;

sign used to mark start of road section reserved for motor vehicles and on which special rules apply (eg motorway rules). May be used also to give advanced warning of such a section if sign contains an inscription giving the distance to the start of a section or has a supplementary sign attached — see *distance to* above (white on blue) (not used in UK)

tramway stop (not used in UK)

bus lane, reserved for the use of buses and cycles (UK sign) (white on blue with black edges)

contra-flow bus lane (UK sign) (white on blue with black edges)

road open or closed; sign used for mountain roads and passes (example given for the Furka Pass, Switzerland).

If the road is closed, panel 1 should display a red sign with the word 'CLOSED' (in several languages) panel 3 should display the name of the place up to which the road is open. If the road is open, panel 1 should display a green sign with the word 'OPEN' (in several languages) and panel 3 should remain blank. Panel 2 should display the following *chains or snow tyres recommended* sign, the above *snow chains compulsory* sign, remain blank or display a sign reading 'open as far as' (only if road is closed) — according to the road conditions. Panels 2 and 3 should be in black on white ground (not used in UK).

chains or snow tyres recommended (black on white ground) (not used in UK)

first aid station (red cross on white square on blue or green ground) (not used in UK)

breakdown service (dark blue or black symbol on white or yellow rectangle on blue or green ground) (not used in UK)

telephone (colours as for above sign)

filling station (colours as for above sign)

hotel or **motel** (colours as for above sign)

restaurant (colours as for above sign)

refreshments or **cafeteria** (colours as for above sign)

Note: The above four symbols frequently form part of other signs.

picnic site (colours as for above sign)

youth hostel (colours as for above sign)

starting point for walks (colours as for above sign) (not used in UK)

tourist information (UK sign) (black 'i' and white on blue ground)

camping site (colours as for above sign)

historic property regularly open to the public; two alternative signs (black symbol on white rectangle on blue ground) (UK sign)

caravan site (colours as for above sign)

limited duration parking zone (a red and blue 'parking prohibited' sign on a light-coloured field)

camping site and caravan site (colours as for above sign)

parking; an additional notice below this sign may give details of the location or nature of the parking allowed (white 'P' on blue ground)

Although there has been an increasing use of international symbols in US traffic signs, there remain substantial differences between American and European traffic signs.

In the United States, traffic regulatory signs are generally square or rectangular with the longer dimension vertical, and warning signs are generally diamond shaped. Regulatory signs are black or red on a white background – red normally indicating 'stop', 'yield' or a prohibition. Warning symbols are mostly displayed in black on a yellow background, although warning and guidance symbols connected with construction and maintenance operations are displayed in black on an orange background. Green is used on signs indicating permitted movement or giving directional guidance, and blue is used on signs indicating motorist services. Brown and white signs give information mainly for public recreational guidance.

REGULATORY SIGNS

Note: The signs in this section are black on a white field, unless otherwise stated.

stop (white on red)

yield (white on red)

do not enter (white on red)

no left turn (black and white with red circle and bar)

no right turn (black and white with red circle and bar)

no U turn (black and white with red circle and bar)

left turn only; a mirror-image of this sign implies 'right turn only'

left or through; a mirror-image of this sign implies 'right or through'

keep right; a mirror-image of this sign implies 'keep left'

two-way left turn lane

no trucks (black and white with red circle and bar)

no bicycles (black and white with red circle and bar)

no parking (black and white with red circle and bar)

no pedestrians (black and white with red circle and bar)

no hitchhiking (black and white with red circle and bar)

restricted lane

one-way traffic

divided highway

tow-away zone

truck weight limit

reserved parking for handicapped (white international 'handicapped' symbol on blue square; remainder of symbol green on white)

WARNING SIGNS

Note: The signs in this section are black on a yellow field, unless stated otherwise.

right turn; a mirror-image of this sign implies 'left turn'

right curve; a mirror-image of this sign implies 'left curve'

right reverse turn; a mirror-image of this sign implies 'left reverse turn'

winding road (right); a mirror-image of this sign implies 'winding road (left)'

HIGHWAY SIGNS 2

sharp curve to left

roadway alignment

crossroad

side road (left); a mirror-image of this sign implies 'side road (right)'

Y intersection

T intersection

stop ahead (black and yellow sign with a red octagon)

yield ahead (black and yellow sign with a small white triangle and a red triangle)

signal ahead (black and yellow sign with the light signals shown in red, yellow and green)

merging traffic (from right); a mirror-image of this sign implies merging traffic from left

added lane (from right); a mirror-image of this sign implies added lane from left

two-way traffic

fire station

road narrows (from right); a mirror-image of this sign implies road narrows from left

hill

hill (bicycle)

divided highway

divided highway ends

slippery (when wet)

handicapped crossing

playground

low vertical clearance

narrow bridge

pavement ends

truck crossing

snowmobile crossing

equestrian crossing

farm machinery crossing

cattle crossing

HIGHWAY SIGNS 2

deer crossing

pedestrian crossing

bicycle crossing

school zone

school crossing

workers ahead (black on orange)

flagger ahead (black on orange)

low shoulder (black on orange)

GUIDE SIGNS

interstate route marker (white letters and numbers on a red and blue sign)

US route marker (black and white)

county route marker (yellow on blue)

forest route marker (white on brown)

interchange exit (white on green)

mile marker (white on green)

bicycle route marker (white on green)

bicycle route (white on green)

airport (white on green)

bus station (white on green)

train station (white on green)

STATE HIGHWAY ROUTE MARKERS

Note: The signs in this section are designed by each state. They are black and white, unless otherwise stated.

Alabama

Alaska

Arizona

Arkansas

California (green on white)

Colorado (a motif of a red 'C', with a black outline, around a yellow disk, on blue and white stripes; the remainder of the sign in black and white)

Connecticut

HIGHWAY SIGNS 2

Delaware

Florida

Georgia

Hawaii

Idaho

Illinois

Indiana

Iowa

Kansas (black and yellow)

Kentucky

Louisiana (green on white)

Maine

Maryland

Massachusetts

Michigan

Minnesota (white numbers on blue and yellow sign)

Mississippi

Missouri

Montana

Nebraska

Nevada

New Hampshire

New Jersey

New Mexico (black and white sign with red circular motif)

HIGHWAY SIGNS 2

New York **60**

North Carolina **12**

North Dakota N D **6**

Ohio **93**

Oklahoma **50**

Oregon **99**

Pennsylvania **39**

Rhode Island R.I. **10**

South Carolina S.C. **3**

South Dakota (black numbers on white and green) **34**

Tennessee **76**

Texas **6** TEXAS

Utah

Vermont

Virginia

Washington

West Virginia

Wisconsin

Wyoming (black on yellow)

SERVICE SIGNS

Note: The signs in this section are white on blue.

gas (petrol)

diesel

food

lodging

telephone

hospital

151

HIGHWAY SIGNS 2

camping (trailer or caravan)

camping (tent)

trailer (caravan) **sanitary station**

rest area

access for handicapped

information

RECREATION SIGNS
Note: The signs in this section are white on brown, unless otherwise stated.

winter recreation area

marina

viewing area

rest rooms

food service

post office

mechanic

ferry

boat launching ramp

first aid (white and brown with red cross)

sail boating (sailing)

parking

water skiing

swimming

ice skating

canoeing

snow skiing

motor boating

fishing

HIGHWAY SIGNS 2

ranger station

amphitheatre

no smoking (white and brown with red diagonal bar)

picnic area

campfires

public parking (green on white)

hiking trail (white on green)

detour (orange and black)

no passing zone (black on yellow)

must exit lane (black on yellow)

railroad advance crossing (black on yellow)

MISCELLANEOUS SIGNS

bus stop (red, black and white)

railroad crossing (black and white)

Hydrogeological maps and sections are drawn to show groundwater resources, and, where necessary, surface water features, in relation to the topography and geology of an area.

The following symbols conform to those given in the *International Legend for Hydrogeological Maps* published by UNESCO (1970). The committee and working group for the project included representatives from France, West Germany, Hungary, Morocco, the Netherlands, UK, USA and USSR.

Although these symbols may be used in black and white, colours are frequently employed to aid clarity. The *International Legend for Hydrogeological Maps* recommends the use of the following colours for different types of information or feature:

grey   topography
black   geological contacts (or colours conforming to international usage)
brown   lithology (unless colours are used to indicate specific geological
          formations)
blue   natural surface-water features
orange   hydrochemical information
red   man-made features

Certain of the general geological and lithological symbols given in *Geology* may be found used in conjunction wth the symbols in this section. Geological symbols given here are specific to hydrogeological maps.

GEOLOGICAL FEATURES
Note: These symbols are in black unless stated otherwise.

contour lines showing height or depth of formation (top or base) relative to national reference level. Line broken or queried where uncertain. Colour black, but green or colour of geological formation if symbol may be confused with other geological symbols.

———22———

Note: On special maps, the thickness (in metres) or depth of the **saturated zone of an aquifer** or water-bearing bed of strata may be shown by the above symbol (see *Groundwater Features* below).

thin impermeable bed between two permeable formations. Continuous line indicating extent of outcrop, dotted line indicating extent concealed bed. Colour should be that of geological formation.

Note: Impermeable formations may be indicated by a light wash in colour of the geological formation.

belt of fractured rock from which water can be obtained

(zig-zag in black, other lines in violet or, if water is saline, orange)

fault, hydrogeological characteristics unknown

fault acting as a conduit

groundwater moves across fault

fault acts as barrier

Note: The triangle in the above three symbols may be drawn in violet with the line and arrow(s) indicating the fault location in black.

HYDROGEOLOGY

NATURAL SURFACE-WATER FEATURES

Note: These symbols are in blue, if coloured, unless stated otherwise.

perennial stream with direction of flow; line thicker where discharge is larger

Note: A highly **saline stream** may be indicated by an orange margin on either side of the above stream symbol; while a highly (organically) **polluted stream** may be indicated by a grey margin on either side.

seasonal stream with direction of flow

intermittent stream with direction of flow; on maps of arid zones the frequency of flowing should be indicated.

disappearance point of stream or point at which it loses water

marsh, permanent or temporary

Note: A **salt marsh** may be indicated by the above symbol in orange.

area inundated during floods

boundaries of known floods; frequency, periods and dates of floods should be indicated

4-5-1920 (approx. 10 yr. flood)

7-3-1953 (approx. 50 yr. flood)

12-7-1942 (approx. 100 yr. flood)

surface-water divide • • • • • •

spring (small-scale maps) ●

spring (large-scale maps)

alternative to above two symbols (also **borehole** or **well,** see *Man-made Features* below)

hydrodynamical data applied to outside of spring symbol (example) —
1 = filing number,
2 = temperature,
3 = altitude,
4 = discharge

group of springs

natural pond or **waterhole,** with no outlet (also **reservoir,** see *Man-made Features* below)

Note: The chemical composition of water in ponds, waterholes or springs may be indicated by the appropriate symbol being drawn with a double outline and one of the colours given under *chemical composition* (see *Hydrochemistry* below)

lake (with lines parallel to shore as shown, or in full colour; boundary dotted where intermittent)

Note: A **salt lake** may be indicated by a blue line with an orange margin on the inner (lake) side.

glacier

GROUNDWATER FEATURES

Note: These symbols are in violet, if coloured, unless stated otherwise.

direction of groundwater flow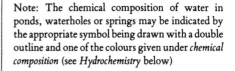

groundwater divide o o o o o o

boundary of **area with confined groundwater** + + + + + +

boundary of **area of artesian flow;** data (if known) shown on artesian side of boundary

1967
||||||||||||||||||

groundwater barrier within an aquifer (large-scale and special maps)

—+——+——+—

natural replenishment of groundwater (in mm per year — figures in violet)

350

height or **depth of water level** relative to the national grid at a given time or **average depth to water table** as lines of equal depth, normally in colour of formation; or, with line in colour of formation and figures in red, **thickness of saturated zone of aquifer** (also **contour line,** see *Geological Features* above)

——26——

alternatives to the above symbol; broken or queried where uncertain; different line ornaments for different aquifers

— —75 — —? —

———70————?———

— —120— —·——?—

·———90———·——?—

Note: The following features may be indicated by use of line, pattern and colour, as specified.

infiltration conditions of covering layers may be indicated by patterns chosen by the cartographer

transmissivity may be indicated by lines of equal transmissivity in pale colours (large-scale and special maps)

average yield of wells may be indicated by a range of shades of one colour, greater intensity indicating greater yield, or by lines of equal specific capacity (large-scale and special maps)

exploitable yields of an aquifer (per unit of its development area) may be indicated by a range of shades of violet (large-scale and special maps)

aquifer in porous formation(s) may be indicated by one of two shades of blue — greater intensity implying an extensive and productive aquifer; lesser intensity implying local or discontinuous aquifer (small-scale maps)

aquifer in fissured formation(s) may be indicated by one of two shades of green — the greater intensity of green implying the greater yield (small-scale maps)

regions without groundwater or with very local groundwater (permeability low to very low) may be indicated by one of two shades of brown — the greater intensity of brown implying the greater yield (small-scale maps)

HYDROCHEMISTRY

Note: These symbols are in orange, if coloured, unless stated otherwise.

total dissolved solids or total chloride or total hardness, etc of groundwater may be indicated by lines of equal concentration, broken where uncertain; or a range of shades in cross-sections on special maps. (Contour lines and depth of water level, see above, are represented in a similar way.)

——3—— - - -

depth of interface between fresh and saline groundwater below the national reference level (contour line broken where uncertain)

══9══ ═ ═

water temperature in degrees Celsius (example); figures and symbol may be in orange

55°

Note: **Chemical composition of groundwater** may be indicated by shades or lines of equal concentration in the following colours (bi-coloured stripes representing mixed features):

Bicarbonate water
calcium   light blue
magnesium   violet-blue
sodium   dark (Prussian) blue

HYDROGEOLOGY

Sulphate water
calcium   yellow
magnesium   orange
sodium   yellow-brown

Chloride water
calcium   green-brown
magnesium   blue-green
sodium   green

MAN-MADE FEATURES

Note: These symbols are in red, if coloured, unless stated otherwise.

borehole or **well,** general symbol, or **non-artesian well** (also **spring,** see *Natural Surface-water Feaures* above)

artesian well, not overflowing

artesian well, overflowing

recharge well

dry well

drilled well (large-scale or special maps)

Note: The above symbols may imply a group of wells if drawn large in relation to other well symbols. Hydrochemical data may be indicated by the above symbols being drawn with a double outline and one of the colours given in *chemical composition* (above) applied within the inner circle. Various forms of stripe and infill to the inner circle may be used to indicate the amount of chemical present.

shaft

alternative to above symbol

mouth of **mining gallery**

spring used for supply (if coloured, square is red, spring symbol is blue)

alternative to above symbol (if coloured, square is red, spring symbol is blue)

drainage gallery

groundwater observation station, without recorder

groundwater observation station, with recorder

groundwater observation station, decade station

gauging station on stream with yearly average flow and area of catchment; additional information may be given inside symbol (if coloured, symbol for station is red, stream is blue)

gauging station (decade station) on stream (if coloured, symbol for station is red, stream is blue)

cistern or other underground reservoir

surface reservoir (also **natural pond,** see *Natural Surface-water Features* above)

pipeline for water (on maps of arid zones only)

dam, example indicating a capacity of 30 million m³

dam, with hydro-electric station

underground dam

canal, irrigation canal — perennial waters

canal — flood waters

drainage canal

Mathematical symbols are understood internationally.

The symbols in this section fall into two categories: the first those containing symbols employed in many fields of mathematics, and the second those containing symbols specific to particular fields. Note that certain symbols change meaning from one specific field to another.

Where a symbol is only recognizable in context or where the arrangement of figures is itself symbolic, the letters a, A, b, B, and c, C have been used to indicate the normal locations of the various elements forming the arrangement. As used in this section, these letters have no other significance.

For symbols used in logic circuit diagrams, see *Electronics*.

GENERAL INSTRUCTIONS AND LABELS

plus, add $+$

eg $4 + 6 = 10$

also denotes **positive,** eg $+ a$

See also *Set Notation* and *Mathematical Symbolic Logic* below.

minus, subtract $-$

eg $5 - 4 = 1$

also denotes **negative** eg $- a$

plus or minus $\pm$

eg $\sqrt{16} = \pm 4$

divide, divided by $\div$

eg $20 \div 5 = 4$

Note: Also shown by a horizontal or diagonal line implying the number above the line (a) is to be divided by the number below (b) – a fraction. $\dfrac{a}{b}$

eg a half or 1 divided by 2 $\dfrac{1}{2}$

multiply, multiplied by, times x

eg $6 \times 4 = 24$

except for the **Cartesian product** (set notation) eg the Cartesian product of X and Y $(X \times Y)$

Note: Where the meaning is clear, the above symbol may be omitted, ie 'a x b' may be written 'ab' or 'a.b'.

the **root** of, the number that when multiplied by itself the number of times specified by the small figure (b) would equal the figure in (a) $\sqrt[b]{a}$

eg the cube (3rd) root of 8 (= 2) $\sqrt[3]{8}$

the **square root** of, the 2nd root. No small figure is given in (b) as above. $\sqrt{a}$

eg $\sqrt{16} = \pm 4$

factorial, the product of the so labelled integer and all lower integers $!$

eg factorial 6 or 6 factorial, $= 6 \times 5 \times 4 \times 3 \times 2 \times 1 = 720$ $6!$

MATHEMATICS

sigma (Greek), add together all the, the summation of Σ

eg use of sigma meaning add together all elements (terms) labelled a between the limits of a and a, ie $a+a+a+a+a$. The locations of the group or series label (a), the generalized suffix (b), the lower limit (3) and the upper imit (7) are typical.

$$\sum_{b=3}^{7} ab$$

the **arithmetic mean**, the average $\overline{x}$

eg $\overline{x}$ of 3, 5, 7, 9,

$$\overline{x} = \frac{3+5+7+5}{4} = \frac{24}{4} = 6$$

the **standard deviation** (Greek), the square root of the average of the squared deviations measured from the mean. It is a measure of dispersion within a set of data. σ

the **standard error of the mean,** the standard deviation divided by the square root of a total number of data-items under consideration. It is a measure of dispersion from the arithmetic mean. $\overline{\sigma}$

the **limit** when one element (a) approaches a specific value (b) $a\overset{L}{\rightarrow}b$

per cent, hundredth parts of a whole %

eg five per cent, five out of a total one hundred parts 5%

EQUALS, INEQUALITIES AND OTHER COMMON RELATIONSHIPS

is **equal** to, equals $=$

eg $7 + 5 = 12$

is **not equal** to $\neq$

eg $7 + 7 \neq 12$

is **approximately equal** to $\mathbin{\triangleq}$

eg $121 \div 6 \mathbin{\triangleq} 20$

alternative to above symbol $\simeq$

alternative to above symbol $\doteqdot$

alternative to above symbol $\fallingdotseq$

is **nearly equal** to $\approx$

eg $\pi^2 \approx 9{\cdot}8696$

is **congruent** with (in reference to numbers), has the same remainder when divided by the modulus as $\equiv$

eg 26 and 16 are congruent, modulus 5 (because $26 \div 5$ and $16 \div 5$ both have the remainder of 1) $26 \equiv 16 (\text{mod.}5)$

is **congruent** with (in geometry), is identical in size and shape $\equiv$

eg triangle ABC is identical to triangle DEF $\triangle ABC \equiv \triangle DEF$

is **not congruent** with (in geometry or in reference to numbers) $\not\equiv$

is **greater than** $>$

eg 5 is greater than 3 $5 > 3$

MATHEMATICS

is **greater than or equal to** $\geqslant$

eg a is greater than or equal to 3

$$a \geqslant 3$$

alternative to above symbol $\geq$

is **less than** $<$

eg 5 is less than 9 $5 < 9$

is **less than or equal to** $\leqslant$

eg b is less than or equal to 9 $b \leqslant 9$

alternative to above symbol $\leq$

to, used to denote a **ratio** (the proportion of one element to another)

eg 1 part of cement to every 2 parts of sand to every 3 parts of aggregate

$$\text{cement: sand: aggregate} = 1:2:3$$

such that (in set notation) $:$

eg a set of the cs such that c is less than 5 $\{c:c<5\}$

INDICES AND SUFFIXES

an **exponential**, power, index; the number of times a number or term (a) is to be multiplied by itself is given by the raised figure (b) a^b

eg
$$(3+2)^3$$
$$= 5^3$$
$$= 5 \times 5 \times 5$$
$$= 125$$

the **complement of the set,** A^1
see *Set Notation* below

the **negation** of the specified statement (a) (in mathematical symbolic logic) a^1

---

a **suffix,** the small letter or number (b) identifies the subject or value to which the element (a) is being specifically referred a_b

eg Let W = the weight of any cake.
Let W_1 = weight of 1st cake,
W_2 = weight of 2nd cake,
W_3 = weight of 3rd cake.
Then average weight of the three cakes $= \dfrac{W_1 + W_2 + W_3}{3}$.

reference suffix; the suffix defines the position (relative to one particular term) of a term in a series a_b a_{b-c} a_{b+c}

eg If, describing fuel consumption, we let F = fuel consumption, F_t = fuel consumption during a chosen period of time, then F_{t-1} would symbolize fuel consumption during the previous period, F_{t+1} fuel consumption during the following period.

a **matrix element reference** defines an element from a table or matrix of similarly labelled elements by its row number (b) and its column number (c) a_{bc}

eg Let the table opposite be a table of m values, then m_{32} is 5.

14	9	10	15	22
8	17	15	12	13
7	5	8	11	9
16	19	16	10	21

alternative forms of above symbol $a_{b.c}$ $a_{b,c}$

definite integral, the range limits defined by lower limit (figure – a) and upper limit (figure – b) see *Calculus* below $\int_a^b$

MATHEMATICS

BRACKETS

a pair of **brackets** placed around (before or after) part of an expression implies that the bracketed part should be **considered as having a single entity**. In general, any operation carried out on or with a bracketed section must act on or with all terms within the brackets. If possible, any operation enclosed within brackets is to be carried out prior to the remainder of the expression. Where one pair of brackets is enclosed by another, the innermost operation is to be carried out first. For clarity, the outer pair of brackets is normally drawn larger or as large **square brackets** as shown opposite.

( )

[ ]

eg

$$a\ [b(a+c)-c(a+b)]$$
$$= a(ba+bc-ca-cb)$$
$$= a^2b+abc-a^2c-abc$$
$$= a^2b-a^2c$$

a **vector** may be denoted by a pair of brackets around a list of numbers or symbols (a horizontal list denotes a row vector, a vertical list a column vector) eg

(a c b d)

$$\begin{bmatrix} a \\ c \\ b \\ d \end{bmatrix}$$

a **matrix** may be denoted by brackets around a table (rectangular array) of numbers or symbols eg

$$\begin{pmatrix} a\ d\ b\ c \\ B\ a\ c\ d \\ c\ b\ a\ B \end{pmatrix}$$

the probability of

P( )

eg, could be used to indicate the probability of drawing a heart from a pack of cards

P(heart)

the possible **number of combinations** that can be made out of a number (a) taking a certain number (b) at a time

$$\begin{pmatrix} a \\ b \end{pmatrix}$$

brackets specifically to enclose **a definition of a set** are drawn as right or similar. For example of use see *such that* in *General Words and Phrases* below. Also may be used as an alternative to square brackets (see above).

{ }

POINTS

decimal point, placed at midpoint or on base line between the units digit and the decimal fraction

eg

15·47
or 15.47

recurring decimal, point placed above part of decimal fraction that repeats

eg

$$\frac{1}{9} = ·11\dot{1}$$

$$\frac{1}{11} = ·09\dot{0}\dot{9}$$

(or ·09̇09̇)

differentiation in respect to time, point placed over a letter, see *Calculus* below

$\dot{C}$

and so on, implies that the preceding sequence continues indefinitely

. . . .

eg

$$\pi = 3·14159. . . .$$

or the preceding established pattern continues to a stated value or term eg

$$1 + 2 + 3 + 4 . . . . + 100$$

therefore, see *General Words and Phrases* below $\therefore$

because, see *General Words and Phrases* below $\because$

to (used to denote a **ratio**) or **such that** (in set notation), see *Equals, Inequalities and Other Common Relationships* above $:$

multiply, multiplied by, one term (a) times another term (b) (alternative to normal symbol $\times$) $a.b$

GENERAL WORDS AND PHRASES

therefore $\therefore$
eg $a^2 = b$
$\therefore a = \sqrt{b}$

because $\because$
eg $\because a^2 = b$
$a = \sqrt{b}$

implies, implies that, then, ie one can infer from one statement the truth of a second statement but not necessarily the truth of the first statement from the second $\Rightarrow$
eg $a^2 = b$
$\Rightarrow \sqrt{b} = a$

alternative to above symbol $\rightarrow$

tends to, approaches limit, becomes (see *limit* in *General Instructions and Labels* above) $\rightarrow$

implies and is implied by, if and only if; commonly used in set notation $\Leftrightarrow$

eg, y is an element of the intersection of sets A and B if and only if y is an element of set A and y is an element of set B $y \in (A \cap B)$
$\Leftrightarrow y \in A$ and $y \in B$

such that, commonly used in set notation $\|$

eg, a set of all the xs such that x is less than 9 and greater than 5 $\{x \| 9 > x > 5\}$

alternative to above symbol, see *Points* above $:$

is parallel to, $\|$
eg, line AB is parallel to line CD $AB \| CD$

CONSTANTS

infinity ∞

Pi (Gk, lc), $= 3 \cdot 14159265 ...$, the ratio of the circumference of a circle to its diameter π

exponential e, e
$2 \cdot 71828....$, $e = \dfrac{1}{1!} + \dfrac{1}{2!} + \dfrac{1}{3!} + 1....$

CALCULUS

delta (Greek), a portion more of Δ
eg, delta A ΔA

delta (Greek), an infinitesimal increment of δ

MATHEMATICS

alternative to above symbol ∂

Note: The above symbol is used in partial derivatives as in the following example:

partial derivative of z with respect to x with y held constant, where z = (z,y)

$\left(\dfrac{\partial z}{\partial x}\right) y$

a **function** of, ie a variable quantity in constant relation to

f

eg, A is a function of B, ie the value of A depends on the value of B

$A = f(B)$

alternative to above symbol

F

the **first derivative** of the function B = f·(a), ie the rate of change of one factor (B) in relation to another factor (a)

$\dfrac{dB}{da}$

Note: Higher derivatives may be indicated by a numeric suffix:

$\dfrac{d^n B}{d a^n}$

differential suffix indicates suffixed function (C) has been differentiated

C'

eg, where B = 2a², then $\underline{d\,B} = 4a = B^1$
      da

$B'(a)$

Note: Higher derivatives may be indicated by repeating the above mark; eg,

$B'''(a)$

the **integral** of, integrate; used commonly in the following two contexts:

$\int$

the **indefinite integral** of function A with respect to variable b where A = f(b)

$\int Adb$

eg
$$\int 6x + 4dx = 3x^2 + 4x - k$$
              where k is a constant

---

the **definite integral** of function C = f(B) between the limits of B = a and B = b

$\int_a^b CdB$

eg

$$\int_1^2 6x + 4dx = \underbrace{(3x^2 + 4x + k)}_{x=2} - \underbrace{(3x^2 + 4x + k)}_{x=1}$$
$$= (12 + 8 + k) - (3 + 4 + k)$$
$$= 20 + k - 7 - k$$
$$= 13$$

GEOMETRY

right angle, 90°, one line perpendicular to another

angle

equal angles can be indicated by similar multiples of the angle symbol

eg, two congruent triangles

degree, 360th of a circle

°

eg, 60 degrees

60°

minute, 60th of a degree (may also indicate **foot**)

′

eg, three minutes

3′

second, 60th of a minute (may also indicate **inch**)

″

eg, five degrees, eight minutes and 30 seconds

5°8′30″

Note: Fractions of a degree may be indicated by use of the decimal point; eg, 56°15′ may be referred to as 56.25°.

triangle	△
eg, triangle ABC	△ABC

parallel (symbol used on a line as in example), see also *parallel* in *General Words and Phrases* above   >

eg, two parallel lines

diameter (Greek) ϕ

radius (Greek) ρ

GRAPH CONVENTIONS

the **Cartesian Coordinate System** (after René Descartes 1596-1650), a two-dimensional system used to show the relationship between two factors.

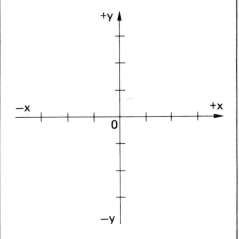

Horizontal distances represent x values, vertical distances represent y values: the further to the right of zero, the greater the x positive; the further to the left, the greater the x negative; the further above zero, the greater the y positive, the further below, the greater the y negative.

a **'3-dimensional' system**, in common use, is developed from the above to represent the relationship between three factors.

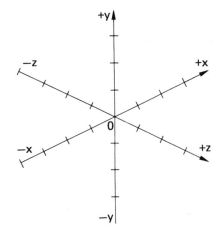

The greater the positive value of the third factor (z), the greater the distance behind the x/y plane (zero position) and away from the viewer; the greater the negative, the greater the distance from the x/y plane towards the viewer.

alternative form to above **'3-dimensional' system**, with the positive values of the third factor (z) being indicated above the x/y plane

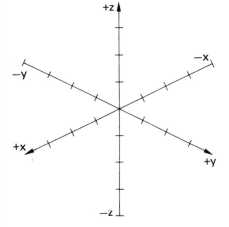

Note: Although more than three dimensions cannot be represented graphically, the Cartesian Coordinate System may be extended (mathematically) to n dimensions.

MATHEMATICS

SET NOTATION

the **universal set**, a set containing all members	U
two alternatives to above symbol	&ₑ E
an **empty set**, a set with no members	∅
alternative to above symbol, ie a pair of set brackets without contents	{ }
is a **subset** of, is a set completely contained within set . . .	⊂
eg, set B is a subset of set A	B⊂A
contains as a subset	⊃
eg, set A contains set B as a subset	A⊃B
is an **element** of, a member of	∈
eg, c is an element of set A	c∈A
contains as an element	∋
eg, set A contains c as an element	A∋c
the **intersection** of, a set containing all members common to	∩
eg, the intersection of sets A and C, ie the set of all elements belonging to both A and C	A∩C
the **union** of, a set containing all members of	∪
eg, the union of sets A and C, ie the set of all elements belonging to either A or C	A∪C

Note: The above symbols ⊂, ⊃, ∈, ∋, ∩ and ∩ may be enlarged and written before the sets they act on, eg, ∩ {A, B, C} means the intersection of sets A, B and C.

not, a diagonal stroke through the above symbols indicates the negative	/
set A is not a subset of set B	A⊄B
the **complement of a set**, a set which contains all members of the universal set which are not in the specified set (A)	A'

Alternative notation for the above symbols is as follows:

the **intersection symbol** is substituted by the normal algebraic notation for 'multiply'

eg, AB, A.B, A(BC)
    mean A∩B, A∩B, A∩ (B∩C)

the union of	+
the universal set	1
the empty set	O

MATHEMATICAL SYMBOL LOGIC

and	∧
eg, both statement a and statement b	a∧b
either or both, or	∨
eg, either statement a or statement b or both statements	a∨b

nor	N		*Abbreviated notation* for the above:	
eg, neither statement a nor statement b	$a_N b$		**and**, the normal algebraic notation for 'multiply' without the sign ' $\times$ '	
the truth value of a **true** statement	1		eg, a and b	ab
			either or both, or	+
the truth value of a **false** statement, ie if a = 1, then $a^1 = 0$ and vice versa	0		**implies and is implied by** (instead of $\Leftrightarrow$), see *General Words and Phrases* above	=
the **negation** of the specified statement (a)	a'			

The items in this section marked 'USGS' conform with symbols given in the *List of Geologic Map Symbols* (1977) published by the United States Geological Survey. Those marked 'BMR' conform with symbols given in a standard range of symbols compiled by the staff of the Australian Bureau of Mineral Resources.

The symbols in this section may be used with appropriate general geological symbols (see *Geology*).

GENERAL SYMBOLS AND OPEN/ SURFACE WORKS

open cut, quarry, trench, prospect pit or **glory hole**; subject indicated by particular shape and size of symbol drawn on map (USGS, BMR)

strip mine (USGS)

prospecting pit, figure giving depth (BMR)
 3

trench, symbol for small-scale maps (USGS)

small prospect pit or **open cut**, for small-scale maps (USGS)

prospect with little or no production (BMR)

mine (BMR); USGS recommends that this symbol should also imply **quarry, glory hole** or **large open pit** on small-scale maps

open cut, quarry (BMR)

sand, gravel or clay pit (BMR), on small-scale maps only (USGS)

Note: The above four symbols encircled imply a major mine or quarry, or struck through imply a mine or quarry not being worked (BMR).

dump (USGS, BMR)

smelter, battery or other **treatment plant**; may be struck through to indicate 'not operating' (BMR)

sample line, type of sample may be indicated by letters, eg c – channel, h – chip, b – bulk (BMR)

grab sample locality (BMR)

drill hole, showing projection in horizontal plane and inclination downwards (arrow reversed for hole drilled upwards), numerals and letters examples only (BMR)

vertical drill hole, example indicating diamond drill and depth in metres (BMR)
DD○50

Note: The following abbreviations may be used with the above two symbols (BMR):

DD   diamond drill
HD   hand drill
PD   percussion drill
RD   rotary drill

UNDERGROUND WORKINGS
including openings at surface

vertical shaft at surface (USGS) or extending below plan level (BMR)

shaft extending above plan level (BMR)

shaft extending above and below plan level (BMR, USGS)

bottom of shaft (USGS)

inclined shaft (BMR)

inclined shaft opening at surface (USGS)

inclined shaft, on small-scale maps (USGS, BMR)

shaft – inaccessible (BMR)

inclined workings, chevrons point down (USGS)

head of raise or winze (USGS, BMR)

raise or winze extending through level (USGS)

foot of raise or winze (USGS) or **raise or winze extending through level** (BMR)

foot of raise or winze (BMR)

portal of tunnel or adit (USGS, BMR)

portal of tunnel or adit, on small-scale maps (USGS, BMR)

cross-section of **cross-cut or drive**, same side of plan of section as observer (BMR)

cross-section of **cross-cut or drive**, opposite side of plan of section from observer (BMR)

cross-section of **cross-cut or drive**, extending across plane of section (BMR)

elevation of roof or back (USGS)

elevation of floor or sill (USGS)

ore chute (BMR)

stoped area, on plan (BMR)

Stoped above

stoped area, in section (USGS, BMR)

alternative to above symbol (BMR)

Stope

lagging or **cribbing** along drive, etc (BMR)

lagging or **cribbing** along drift (USGS)

workings caved-in or otherwise inaccessible (USGS, BMR)

filled workings (BMR)

MINING

natural surface in sections, where lithology and dip of strata is not shown (BMR)

information projected onto a section from near side (BMR)

information projected onto a section from far side (BMR)

The following symbols denote the monetary units used in currency notes, coinage, price labelling, accounts and other commercial documentation. For monetary units, other than those given below, abbreviations are frequently employed; eg DM = Deutsch Mark (West Germany), L = Lira (Italy), p = pence (UK). See also *Commerce*.

colon(s), monetary unit of Costa Rica and El Salvador   ₡

dollar(s), primarily the monetary unit of USA but also of Antigua (East Caribbean $), Australia, Bahamas, Barbados, Belize, Bermuda, British Virgin Isles (US $), Brunei, Canada, Cayman Islands, Dominica (East Caribbean $), Fiji, Granada (East Caribbean $), Guam (US $), Guyana, Hong Kong, Jamaica, Kiribati (Australian $), Liberia, Nauru (Australian $), New Zealand, Pitcairn Islands (New Zealand $), Puerto Rico (US $), St Christopher (East Caribbean $), St Lucia (East Caribbean $), St Vincent (East Caribbean $), American Samoa (US $), Singapore, Solomon Islands, Taiwan, Turks and Caicos (US $), Tuvalu (Australian $), Vanuatu (Australian $), Virgin Islands (US $), Zimbabwe $

alternatives to above symbol $ $

cent(s), one hundredth of a dollar   ¢

alternatives to above symbol   c ¢

peso(s), the monetary unit of Argentina, Bolivia, Chile, Cuba, Dominican Republic, Guinea Bissau, Mexico, Philippines, Uruguay   ₱

pound(s), primarily pound(s) sterling, ie the monetary unit of Great Britain, but also the monetary unit of Cyprus, Egypt, Falkland Islands, Gibraltar, Irish Republic, Lebanon, Malta, Pitcairn Islands (£ sterling), St Helena, Sudan, Syria   £

alternatives to above symbol   £

real or **reis** (plural), former Portuguese and Brazilian monetary unit   ₨

solidus; used to indicate shilling(s) in former British currency, eg 2/6d (two shillings and six pence); a simplification of the long s (∫). The solidus was a gold coin introduced under the Roman emperor Constantine.   /

Note: The abbreviation 's' was used as an alternative to the above symbol to indicate shilling(s). The abbreviation 'd', used to indicate British pence prior to the introduction of decimal currency, was derived from 'denarius' – a Roman coin.

yen, monetary unit of Japan   ¥

alternative to above symbol   ¥

MUSIC

This section contains the symbols commonly found in conventional Western musical notation which has become generally accepted as the standard means of writing music throughout the world. There are, however, many other musical notation systems in use: some are traditional and others have been more recently devised for specific purposes by *avant-garde* composers and ethnomusicologists, as teaching aids and as attempts at improvements on the present conventions.

Conventional Western musical notation has evolved as a means of issuing instructions from writer to performer with a primary regard to defining sequence, timing and pitch of notes. Essentially, the notes are written in order of performance from left to right, the duration of each note indicated by the form of the note symbol and its pitch by the location of the symbol on, or in relation to, the stave (five horizontal lines). There are few means of defining the timbre or the means of producing the required sounds and the available means of stating variations in pace, accent and volume of sound tend to be imprecise. This can leave considerable choice in interpretation to the performer. The notation's success as a means of communication relies considerably on writer and reader understanding the same musical tradition.

Common versions of the symbols in manuscript form are given where it has been thought useful.

NOTES

breve, twice semibreve length, normally 8 beats

semibreve or whole note (American), normally 4 beats

minim or half note (American), 1/2 semibreve length, normally 2 beats

crotchet or quarter note (American), 1/4 semibreve length, normally 1 beat

quaver or eighth note (American), 1/8 semibreve length, normally 1/2 beat

semiquaver or sixteenth note (American), 1/16 semibreve length, normally 1/4 beat

demi-semiquaver or thirty-second note (American), 1/32 semibreve length, normally 1/8 beat

semi-demi-semiquaver or sixty-fourth note (American), 1/64 semibreve length, normally 1/16 beat

linked notes; pairs and groups of quavers, semiquavers and shorter notes are normally written linked by their 'tails'; eg

a diagonal line above or below a note or chord indicates it is to be performed as **a series of repeated quavers** to equal in total the length of the so-marked note or chord; except for quavers so-marked which are performed as 2 semiquavers; eg

8 quavers

4 quavers

2 semiquavers

two diagonal lines above or below a note or chord indicate it is to be performed as **a series of repeated semiquavers** to equal in total the length of the so-marked note or chord; except for so-marked quavers which are performed as 4 demi-semiquavers; eg

16 semiquavers

4 demi-semiquavers

three diagonal lines above or below a note or chord indicate it is to be performed as **a series of repeated demi-semiquavers** to equal in total the length of the so-marked note or chord; except for so-marked quavers which are performed as 16 demi-semiquavers; eg

16 demi-semiquavers

small size notes written before a standard size note are **ornaments** or **grace notes** ie additional decorative notes (also known as Appogiatura). The small notes (unless crossed with a diagonal line) are played on the beat as if written full size but the following standard size note is reduced to half its written length, the first note is accented; eg

a diagonal line across the tail of the small note indicates it is to be **performed either before or on the beat** (according to musical style) and as quickly as possible before the standard size note which then retains its normal length (also known as Accaciatura); eg

Certain ornaments can be indicated by specific signs, see *Other Signs*.

MUSIC

RESTS OR PAUSES

breve rest, normally 8 beats long

semiquaver rest or sixteenth note rest (American), normally 1/4 beat long

alternative to above symbol

demi-semiquaver rest or thirty-second note rest (American), normally 1/8 beat long

semibreve rest or whole note rest (American), normally 4 beats long

semi-demi-semiquaver rest or sixty-fourth note rest (American), normally 1/16 beat long

minim rest or half note rest (American), normally 2 beats long

long rest lasting the number of bars given by the figure written above the thick line; eg

crotchet rest or quarter note rest (American), normally 1 beat long

quaver rest or eighth note rest (American), normally 1/2 beat long

a six bar rest

STRAIGHT LINES
staves, leger lines, bar-lines, etc

stave; consists of five horizontal lines (in present conventional music). The pitch of a note is indicated by its location on a line or in the space above or below a line; the higher its location on the stave, the higher the pitch of the note – each line and each space implying one interval between adjacent notes on the normal (diatonic) scale (ie ABCDEFGA). The location of a key note, to which all other notes on the stave can be related, is given by the clef, see *Clefs* below; eg

G D E F G A B C D E F G

leger line(s) used to indicate the pitch of a note above or below those notes that can be shown on the stave, ie leger lines are additional short stave lines; eg

G A D C

bar-line(s) vertical lines drawn through the stave(s) to indicate the metrical divisions of the music, ie the bars (or measures), each bar containing a stated number of beats. Usually the first note following a bar-line is emphasized. No bar-line is written before the first note or rest of a piece of music; eg

double bar-line, pair of vertical lines through stave, indicates a change of time signature or key or the end of a section (movement)

repeat sign, double bar-line plus pair of dots either side of centre line indicates repeat a marked section, see *Dots* below

thick and thin vertical lines through stave (also called double bar-line) indicate the end of a piece of music or a repeat

extended bar-line(s), vertical lines linking staves, indicate that the music on the linked staves is to be performed at the same time. Each stave carries the music for one part, voice, instrument or hand (ie in piano playing)

chord repeat; each short, diagonal line is an instruction to repeat the preceding chord once; eg play chord and repeat chord twice

note repeat, diagonal line under or over note(s), see *Notes* above

long rest, see *Rests* above

pedal, direction to pianist to depress right pedal during section indicated by symbol (used above and below stave); eg

Ped.

Ped.

MUSIC

1st time bar and 2nd time bar (or 1st and 2nd endings) signs used above or (inverted) below a repeated section of music to indicate the bar(s) covered by the bracket numbered 1 should be performed once only and omitted in the repeat; eg

CLEFS

Clefs are written in front of the time and key signatures at the beginning of each piece of music, repeated on the lefthand end of each subsequent stave and wherever the locations of the notes on the stave need to be reconfirmed. Each clef gives the location of a key note to which the other notes can be related.

treble or G clef indicates the location of the note G on the second line of the stave. Used for music for higher vocal pitch (soprano, alto and tenor) and instruments that produce notes of that range, and as the higher of the two clefs used for piano music.

or

Note: If used for tenor voice or instrument, the music is performed one octave lower and the clef written as right.

bass or F clef indicates the location of the note F on the fourth line of the stave. Used for music for lower voices and instruments, and as the lower of the two clefs in piano music.

or

tenor clef indicates that the note C is located on the fourth line of the stave. Formerly used for music for tenor voice but superseded by use of treble clef. Now only used for higher range of tenor trombone, cello, bassoon and double bass.

alto clef (the C clef on the middle line) indicates the location of the note C on the third (central) line of the stave. Formerly used for music for alto voice, now only used for music for the viola, being largely superseded by the treble clef.

SHARPS AND FLATS

sharp, written before a note, the symbol indicates the note is to be raised by a semitone (ie sharp) and similarly affects all subsequent notes of that pitch within the same bar, unless contradicted by the natural sign (see below); eg F sharp

written directly after a clef, the sharp symbol implies that all subsequent notes in the same stave location as the symbol are to be raised by a semitone, unless contradicted by the natural sign. Such use of sharp signs (and/or flat signs) is called a *key signature*, ie an indicator of the key of the music; eg **the key of D major**

flat, written before a note, the symbol indicates the note is to be lowered by a semitone (ie flat), and similarly affects all subsequent similarly pitched notes within the same bar, unless contradicted by the natural sign (over); eg **C flat**

written directly after a clef, it implies all subsequent notes in the same stave location as the flat symbol are to be lowered by a semitone, unless contradicted by the natural sign. Such use of flat signs (and/or sharp signs) is called a *key signature*, ie an indicator of the key of the music; eg **the key of E♭ major**

natural or cancel (American), written before a sharp or flat note, it returns it to its normal tone and similarly affects all subsequent similarly pitched notes within the same bar, unless re-marked with a sharp or flat sign; eg

double sharp, written before a note, it raises the note by a whole tone or an already sharp note by a semitone and similarly affects all subsequent notes in the same stave location within the same bar; eg

or ×

natural sharp, written before a note, it contradicts a double sharp and lowers the note by a semitone to sharp; eg

double flat, written before a note, it lowers the note by a whole tone or an already flat note by a semitone and similarly affects all subsequent notes in the same stave location within the same bar; eg

♭♭

natural flat, written before a note, it contradicts a double flat and raises the note by a semitone to flat; eg

♮♭

Note: By convention, the key signature is always followed by the time signature (see *Numbers* below) at the beginning of a piece of music; eg

Flats and sharps forming a key signature are given in a specific order as follows:

F C G D A E B

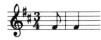
B E A D G C F

F C G D A E B

B E A D G C F

B E A D G C F

NUMBERS

time signature, two numbers, one above the other, written on the stave normally following a clef or a double bar-line. The top number gives the number of beats (not notes) to each bar; the bottom number gives the value of each bar, ie 1 for semibreve, 2 for minim, 4 for crotchet, 8 for quavers, 16 for semiquavers, and so on.

A time signature indicates the rhythm of the music following it. Unless directed otherwise, the main accent falls on the first beat of each bar. With bars of 4 of more beats, there are normally secondary accents; in 4 beat bars, on the 3rd beat; in 6 beat bars, on the 4th beat; in 9 beat bars, on the 4th and 7th beats; in 12 beat bars, on the 4th, 7th and 10th beats; eg

MUSIC

three-four time, meaning each bar contains three beats of crotchet length (with the 1st beat accented), ie waltz time

metronome mark; the exact number of beats to the minute required is given in location x; eg

$\quad$ = x

84 beats to the minute

$\quad$ = 84

couplet or **duplet**; the 2 notes or rests so indicated are performed within the time of 3 notes

triplet; the 3 notes or rests so indicated are performed in the time of 2 notes

or

quadruplet; the 4 notes or rests so indicated are performed in the time of 6 notes

or

quintuplet; the 5 notes or rests so indicated are performed in the time of 4 notes

or

sextuplet; the 6 notes or rests so indicated are performed in the time of 4 notes

or

octave; where symbol is written under note(s), the note(s) are performed an octave higher; where written over note(s), the note(s) are performed an octave lower

8
or 8va
or 8ve

with note an octave lower; where written under or over note(s), the written note(s) and the equivalent note(s) an octave lower are performed together

Con 8va
or Con 8

1st time bar and 2nd time bar signs, see *Straight Lines* above

DOTS

dot(s) following note or rest, one dot **lengthens the note or rest** by half as long again and each additional dot lengthens the note or rest additionally by half as much as the previous dot; eg

$\circ\cdot = \circ + \partial$

$\circ\cdot\cdot = \circ + \partial + \partial$

dot under or over note implies the so-marked note is to be performed **staccato**, ie individually articulated by being slightly shortened to allow for tiny pauses between it and the preceding and following notes; eg

repeat preceding bar, symbol positioned centrally between two bar-lines

repeat preceding two bars, symbol positioned on one bar-line

178

repeat bars contained between these two symbols

bass or F clef, see *Clefs*

sign, used in conjunction with the abbreviation 'DS' (*dal segno* = from the sign) meaning **repeat from the sign**

fermata (from Italian = halt or stop), the note or rest so-marked is held for longer than standard; also used over double bar-line to imply end of music; also known as **pause**

CURVED LINES
brackets, ties, etc

brace linking two or more staves of music to be performed at the same time by one instrument (eg piano or harp) or group of instruments or voices (eg in an orchestral score)

alternative to above symbol

arpeggio (from Italian *arpeggiare* = to play the harp), written in front of a chord to indicate the notes of the chord are to be played rapidly in succession

alternative to above symbol

slur or **tie**; a curved stroke, when written over or under a pair or group of notes of varied pitch, is called a *slur* and indicates the notes are to be played *legato*, ie with each note leading smoothly into the next. Also used to indicate bowing for stringed instruments and, in vocal music, that more than one note is to be sung to one syllable; eg

When under or over notes of the same pitch or similar chords, the curved stroke implies a *tie*, ie indicates the 1st note (or chord) only is performed, but lengthened by the time-value of the following note or chord; used especially to indicate the continuation of a note beyond the end of a bar; eg

OTHER SIGNS

accents; the note so marked is to be emphasized; eg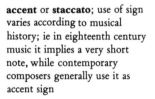

accent or **staccato**; use of sign varies according to musical history; ie in eighteenth century music it implies a very short note, while contemporary composers generally use it as accent sign

up, plucking or bowing symbol for string instruments

down, plucking or bowing symbol for string instruments

MUSIC

trill or **shake**; the so-marked note and the note one tone higher are performed rapidly one after another for as long as the number of beats indicated by the marked note; eg

pralltriller or **inverted mordent**, an ornament; written above a note, implies the rapid repetition of the marked note and the note a tone higher prior to the performance of the marked note – the total duration being that of the marked note; eg

mordent, an ornament; implies the rapid playing of the marked note and the note a tone lower (or, if indicated by use of ♯ or ♭, a semitone lower) prior to the performance of the note – the total duration being that of the marked note; eg

double mordent, an ornament; implies a repeated mordent; eg

turn, an ornament; when written above a note, implies the note a tone above the written note should be performed, followed by the written note, followed by the note a tone below the written note, followed by the written note once more – the total duration being that of the written note; eg

When written between two notes, implies a series of linking notes in the same form as above but following the first note, half its duration and reducing the first note's duration to half; eg

inverted turn, ornament; written above a note, it implies the note a tone below the written note is performed, followed by the written note, followed by the note a tone above the written note, followed by the written note again – the total duration being that of the written note; eg

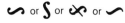 or ∫ or or

crescendo, direction to increase volume of sound

<

diminuendo, direction to decrease volume of sound

>

coda, symbol used to mark the tail-end of a piece of music. *Al coda* means go to the tail-end (the coda).

⊕

COMMON WORDS, PHRASES AND ABBREVIATIONS
used in conjunction with graphic notation

The following list is in alphabetical order. Readily understandable English words have been omitted. The words are generally Italian or Italian in origin – where this is not so the origin has been given. Where the direct translation is not fully applicable to the use of the word(s) in musical notation, the translation has been enclosed by brackets.

a battuta (at the beat), strict time is to be resumed

a capella (at chapel), unaccompanied music for voices

a capriccio (at the caprice), the performer is to decide style and speed of the music

accel see *accelerando*

accelerando, accelerating, increasingly quicker

adagietto (a little *adagio*), not quite as slow as *adagio*

adagio (at leisure), at a slow, comfortable pace

ad lib see *ad libitum*

ad libitum (Latin, at pleasure), the music is to be performed in accordance with the performer's wishes

affettuoso (affectionate), with feeling

affrettando, hastening

agitato, agitated

al coda (to the coda), go to the coda (tail-end of the music – often marked ⊕)

MUSIC

al fine (to the end), go to the end

alla cappella see *a cappella*

allarg see *allargando*

allargando (broadening), becoming broader and slower

alla breve (with the breve), tempo to be twice as fast as that indicated by the note time values

allegretto (a little *allegro*), moderately fast or lively

allegro (merry), at a lively pace

al loco (to the place), see *loco*

all'8va alta (at the octave higher), so-marked section to be performed an octave higher

all'8va bassa (at the octave lower), so-marked section to be performed an octave lower

all'8va sotto see *all'8va bassa*

all'unisono, in unison

al segno (to the sign), go to the sign (normally ✵)

andante (at a walking pace), at a moderate tempo

andantino (a little *andante*), slightly quicker than andante

animato, animated

a piacere (at pleasure), the music may be played in accordance with the performer's choice, especially as to speed

a poco a poco, little by little

a poco più lento, a little more slowly

a poco più mosso, a little more movement, a little quicker

appassionato (enthusiastic, impassioned), to be performed passionately

arco (bow), bowing is to be resumed after a section of plucking (instruction for string instruments)

a tempo (to the tempo), perform in time or return to the original tempo

ben marcato, well marked, see *marcato*

bis (Latin, twice), perform indicated section twice

brillante (brilliant), perform brilliantly – with style

calando (lowering, decreasing), becoming slower and weaker

colla parte (with the part), the accompaniment is to follow the tempo as performed by the soloist

con anima (with spirit), animated

con amore (with love), with tender enthusiasm

con brio, with spirit

con forza, with force, perform strongly

con gracia (with grace), graceful, *grazioso*

con gusto, with zest, enjoyment

con moto (agitation, motion), moving onwards

con sordini, with mutes

con 8 see *Numbers* above

con 8va see *Numbers* above

cresc see *crescendo*

crescendo (growing, increasing), growing in volume

da capo (from the beginning), on reaching the so-marked point, repeat from the beginning

da capo al fine (from beginning to end), on reaching the so-marked point, repeat from the beginning to the word *fine*

dal segno (from the sign), repeat from the sign (normally ✵)

DC see *da capo*

decres see *decresendo*

decresendo (decreasing), growing quieter, *diminuendo*

dim see *diminuendo*

diminuendo (reducing), growing quieter, *decrescendo*

divisi (divided), the music divides into separate parts after a section played in unison, or is divided into separate parts for a group of instruments that normally play in unison

dolce (sweet), sweetly

doppio movimento (double motion), at twice the pace

DS see *dal segno*

DS al coda (from the sign, to the tail-end), repeat from the sign (normally ✵) to the words *al coda*, then go to the tail-end or *coda* (usually marked ⊕)

f, usual sign for *forte*, loudly

ff, usual sign for *fortissimo* (loudest), louder than *f*

fff, louder than *ff*

fine, the end (of the music), may be used prior to the end of the notation to mark the end of the music after repeat(s)

forte see *f*

fp, usual sign for *fortepiano* (loud-soft), implies a sudden change from loud to soft

giocoso, humorous, playful

giusto tempo (proper time), at the proper tempo

gliss see *glissando*

glissando, sliding, ie as the sound produced on a piano or harp by sliding a finger over the keys or strings

grandioso (grand), grandly

grave, serious, heavy, and slow

grazioso, graceful, *con grazia*

larghetto (a little *largo*), slow but not as slow as largo

largo (large, generous, wide), slowly and in noble style

leg see *legato*

legato (tied), performed with each note leading smoothly into the next

leggero (frivolous, light), lightly

leggiero see *leggero*

lento (slow, sluggish), slow

loco (Latin, place), from the so-indicated point onwards, the notes are to be performed as written. (Often used for clarity after section performed an octave higher or lower than normal for remainder of the music.)

maestoso (majestic), stately

maggiore, major, sometimes stated where music returns to major key after section in minor key

marc see *marcato*

marcato, marked, the so-indicated piece is to be performed in a marked manner, or accentuated over accompaniment or other parts

marcia, a march

meno, less, used to qualify other words

mf, usual sign for *mezzo-forte* (half-loud), moderately loud but not as loud as *forte*

mezzo voce (half voice), particular form of quiet singing, also used for instruments to mean 'play in an undertone'

mod see *moderato*

moderato (moderate), moderate pace (also used to qualify words describing pace)

molto, very

mor see *morendo*

morendo, dying away

mosso, moving, animated

mp, usual sign for *mezzo-piano* (half-softly), quietly but not as quietly as *piano*

non, not

non troppo, not too much

8va sotto (octave lower), perform an octave lower

ped, pedal (English), the right pedal on the piano is to be used during so-marked section

perd see *perdendosi*

perdendosi (losing itself), fading away to nothing

p, usual sign for *piano* (softly), quietly

pf, usual sign for *più forte*, more loudly

più, more

pizz see *pizzicato*

pizzicato (pinched), plucked (re string instruments)

poco, little

poco a poco, little by little

pomposo, pompous

pp, usual sign for *pianissimo* (very softly), quieter than *p*

ppp, usual sign for even quieter than *pianissimo*

prestissimo, extremely quickly

presto, quick, fast, faster than *allegro*

rall see *rallentando*

rallentando (slackening), slowing down, *ritardando, ritenuto*

rf, usual sign for *rinforzando*

rinf see *rinforzando*

rinforzando (reinforcing), the note(s) so-marked to be especially accented

rit see *ritenuto*

ritard see *ritardando*

ritardando, retarding, slowing down, *ritenuto, rallentando*

ritenuto (held back), slowing down, *ritardando, rallentando*

segue (follows), implies one section follows on another without a break

semp see *sempre*

sempre, always

senza, without

sf, sfz, usual signs for *sforzando*

sforzando (reinforced), the note(s) so-marked to be especially accented, as *rinforzando*

solo (alone), part so-marked consists of music for one singer or instrument only

soprano, music so-marked is for the highest voices of women (or boys) or instruments which have the same range

sordino, sordini, mute, mutes; music so-marked to be performed with instruments with mutes

MUSIC

sost see *sostenuto*

sostenuto (sustained), the note(s) so-marked to be held for full length

sotto, beneath, under

sotto voce (under voice), music so-marked to be performed in an undertone (as *mezzo voce*)

tacet (Latin, is silent), implies the voice or instrument is to be silent for the so-marked section

tempo (time), pace, speed (of music)

ten see *tenuto*

tenor (English), music so-marked is for the highest, natural vocal range of men or instruments that have that range

tenuto (held), the note(s) so-marked to be held for full length

tr see *trill, Other Signs* above

tranquillo, tranquil, calm

treble (English), music so-marked is for the highest vocal range or instruments that have that range; the term is especially applied to the voices of boys

tre corde (three strings), an instruction in piano music implying the release of the left pedal and a return to normal playing, following a section marked *una corda*

trem see *tremolo*

tremolando (trembling) see *tremolo*

tremolo (quivering), the note or group of notes so-marked is to be rapidly repeated

troppo, much

tutti, all, ie all are to perform; in orchestra scores, sometimes used to imply solo part is to be silent

UC see *una corda*

una corda (one string), in piano music implies the left (damping) pedal is to be used

unison (English), together; notes of the same pitch to be performed together (usually by different voices or instruments)

valse (French), waltz

vibrato, vibrating, quivering; music so-marked to be performed in a vibrant manner. Originally a vocal effect, on string instruments a similar effect is obtained by vibrating a finger on a string as it is played.

vivace, vivacious, lively

vivo (alive) see *vivace*

voce, voice

volti subito see *VS*

VS, usual abbreviation for *volti subito*, turn at once; warning used at bottom of page of music if it is necessary to turn page quickly

The primary purpose of sea or nautical charts is as a navigational aid for shipping. However, they also provide a valuable information source for many other marine activities such as fishing, national defence, oil and gas production, and marine engineering. Normally, land features are given only if thought of interest to mariners. Landmarks visible from the sea should be charted, but the extent and detail given of other land features may vary considerably between charts from different hydrographic bodies.

The symbols and abbreviations in this section conform to the chart specifications adopted as the standard for future national and international charts by the International Hydrographic Organization in April 1981. The specifications were compiled by the following member states of the IHO: Australia, Brazil, Canada, Chile, Denmark, Egypt, France, Germany, Iceland, India, Indonesia, Italy, Japan, Netherlands, New Zealand, Norway, Sweden, UK, USA and USSR. The IHQ recognized that complete international standardization of nautical charts is unlikely to be achieved and so the chart specifications allow for a degree of variation where it was thought that such variation would not mislead a navigator.

Charts conforming with IHO specifications give depths and heights in metres (m) and decimetres (dm), horizontal distances or 'distances on the ground' in nautical miles (M) and cables or metres (m), and velocity in knots (kn). Geographical positions are given in degrees (°), minutes (') and seconds (").

All IHO specification charts are printed in black, blue, buff or grey, and magenta. Most graphic detail, symbols and lettering are printed in black. Blue is used to emphasize areas of shallow water (ie less than five or six metres deep) and certain deeper contours. All land areas are coloured in a 'land' tint of buff or grey, and intertidal areas (ie areas that dry out at low tide) are indicated by an 'intertidal' tint formed by blue overprinted with the land tint. Magenta is used to indicate or emphasize features having a significance beyond their immediate location (eg lights, pilot stations) and non-physical or transitory features (eg restricted areas, ferry routes). On some charts (referred to below as 'multicoloured charts') additional colours may be used; particularly to indicate the colours of red, green and white or yellow lights or light sector limits. White and yellow lights are both indicated by yellow.

The identifying character of a light may be indicated by a sequence of abbreviations. Firstly, the nature or rhythm of the beam or flashes is given by abbreviations such as VQ (very quick), LF (long flash) or F (fixed) and, possibly, a figure or figures in brackets indicating the number of the flashes forming the group or composite group; eg (2 + 3) indicating two flashes followed after a gap, by three flashes. If the light is not white or yellow, this is followed by an abbreviation for the colour; eg R (red), G (green). On multicoloured charts, the colour of lights may be indicated by an appropriately coloured light-flare symbol. The time or period the sequence takes to complete may then be given in seconds (s); which may be followed by the elevation in metres (m) if this is considered important. The elevation of the light may be given from an appropriate high water datum or from mean sea level if there is no appreciable tide at the adjacent shore line. Finally, the approximate, nominal range in sea miles (M) at which the light can be seen, may be given for major lights. The range gives an indication of the brightness of

NAUTICAL CHARTS

the light and is generally estimated assuming a meteorological range or a normal visibility of ten sea miles.

Unfortunately, navigation buoys do not conform to one international buoyage system. In 1975 a technical committee set up by the International Association of Lighthouse Authorities (IALA) in an attempt to harmonize the existing buoyage rules, agreed that there should be two alternative international systems of buoyage: System A (Combined Cardinal and Lateral System – with red to port or the left-hand) and System B (Lateral Systems only – with red to starboard or the right-hand). The implementation of System A began in 1977 and will eventually be introduced throughout the waters of Europe, Africa, and most of Asia and Australasia. System B is to be introduced into American waters and possibly those of Japan and the Phillipines. Cardinal buoys (and beacons) indicate navigable water to the North, East, South or West of themselves as specified by the character of their lights and/or markings. Where System A has been adopted, lateral buoys generally mark the limits to channels with red lighted and coloured buoys marking port-hand limits and green lighted and green or black coloured buoys marking starboard-hand limits for vessels approaching from seaward. Where the lateral system is used away from estuaries or harbour approaches and so the buoyage direction is unclear, the buoyage direction should be indicated by a buoyage direction symbol (see *Buoys, Beacons and Daymarks* below).

HEIGHTS, SOUNDINGS, DEPTHS

Note: Heights and depths are given in metres and decimetres (tenths of a metre). Decimeters are usually indicated by a figure smaller and slightly lower than the associated figures for metres. Examples of height and depth figures are given below. For the significance of colours see introductory note.

height or depth **contour** 500

approximate contour 500

form lines (example); alternative to the use of height contours, giving general form of land (with spot height) $\cdot 70$

precise **spot height** $\cdot 74$

out of position height figures; ie at a distance from located object (12)

height above ground level of tower, chimney etc $\overparen{(30)}$

approximate height of tops of trees, etc where ground level is not visible (example indicating approximate height of 150m) 150

no bottom found at specified depth $\overline{200}$

swept depth, depth cleared by wire drag sweep $\underline{14_8}$

drying height above chart datum $\underline{3}_9$

dredged area or channel (example); in areas not regularly maintained, the year of the latest control survey should be given   Dredged to 6.1m

CONTROL POINTS

fixed **position circle,** general symbol; the dot indicates position of an object or location

approximate position   OPA

Note: Objects thought conspicuous *landmarks* by the cartographer should be identified by being labelled with their names in capital letters. In a symbol representing a specific object, the object's location is normally indicated by a small circle in the symbol's baseline; eg

water tower

triangulation point

observation point for determining precise position by astronomical means

bench mark

GENERAL STRUCTURES ON LAND – including buildings, towers and masts

building or group of buildings (example)

individual **small building**

urban area (example)

Note: Urban areas may also be indicated by the use of hatching or a tint.

post office

church; an indication of whether a church has a spire, twin spires, tower or cupola may be given by a small sketch replacing this symbol or near it or by the abbreviations Tr (tower), Sp (spire), Cup (cupola)

temple, pagoda, shinto shrine or joss house (general symbol)

Buddhist temple or shrine

Note: On large scale charts, a place of worship may be indicated by the outline of the building with one of the above three symbols located over its highest point.

mosque or minaret of a mosque (with the position circle corresponding to the location of the minaret)

radio mast (tall structure held vertical by guy lines)

radio tower (self-supporting lattice structure), or **television mast or tower**

flagpole or flagstaff

chimney stack

flare stack normally showing flames

water tower

NAUTICAL CHARTS

tower; general symbol		**major road**	
monument		**track** or **path**	
windmill		alternative to above symbol	
wind motor (motor structure for the use of wind power)		**cutting**; hachures point down slope	
tank, drawn to scale (example)		**dyke** or **levee**; thinner line to seaward side	
tank, small scale		**embankment** (may be shown with road or rail on crest) or alternative to above symbol	
major fortified structure; castle, fort, large blockhouse, etc; symbol used if structure cannot be drawn to scale		**seawall**; on small-scale charts, a seawall may be shown by above dyke symbol	
minor fortified structure; small fort, battery, 'pillbox', etc; symbol used if structure cannot be drawn to scale		canal or dock **lock**; true to scale outline	
		alternative to above symbol for small-scale representation	

GENERAL ARTIFICIAL FEATURES

railway line (three alternatives)		**dam**; teeth point in direction of flow	
railway station; symbol used where station cannot be drawn to scale		**fixed bridge** or **viaduct**	
rail tunnel		**opening bridge**	
road tunnel		**vertical clearance**, in metres, under bridge, powerline, etc at high water (example)	15
motorway		**horizontal clearance** in metres (example)	⊢15⊣
road			

188

electrical power transmission line

telephone line

overhead transporter or **telepheric**

airfield or **airport**; symbol used where airfield is not drawn to scale

mine or **quarry**

log pond

HARBOURS AND PORTS
including pilot, lifeboat and rescue stations

fishing harbour or **port** (magenta); symbol may be used with other symbols to indicate various fishing features

boat harbour or **marina**

slipways (alternatives)

Slip

Note: On charts that specifically indicate *patent slips* (ie slips with rails for ship cradles), the two parallel lines may be used to identify patent slips and other slipways are then indicated without these parallels but marked with the word 'Slip'.

hard, ramp, causeway

harbour-master's office

custom house

health officer's office or **quarantine building**

position of a **pilot cruising vessel** or position of a meeting or boarding place which a pilot comes out to from shore (magenta)

rescue station or **lifeboat** lying at mooring

tide scale or **gauge**

floating dock; drawn true to scale

alternative to above symbol for minimum size representation

dock or basin entrance with a **caisson** (steel structure which floats or slides into place to close the entrance)

NAUTICAL CHARTS

Note: *Wet docks* and non-tidal basins are normally shown to scale and infilled with blue. *Dry docks* and *floating docks* are not infilled with blue but, to accord with IHO specifications, should be overprinted with land tint. See *General Artificial Features* above for symbols for locks.

gridiron or **careening grid** (flat frame erected on foreshore for ships to dry out on for painting or repair at low water)

dolphin (substantial post(s) or structure for mooring, hauling off vessels and protection of vessels or constructions); large dolphins may be drawn to scale □

deviation dolphin (dolphin which a vessel may swing around for compass adjustment)

Note: *Minor posts* or piles may be indicated by small circles filled in black.

stump of post or pile; the exact position of the stump may be used as an alternative to above symbol

small obstruction; may be used as an alternative to above symbol   Obstn ⬚

timber yard where stacked timber is a prominent feature ♯

crane; cranes may also be indicated by a position circle and legend ⊖

NATURAL TOPOGRAPHIC FEATURES

river or stream; shown by tapering line or two lines with a blue or intertidal tint infill

intermittent stream

rapids and/or **waterfalls** in otherwise navigable river

lake (blue infill)

salt pans

glacier

lava flow (land tint)

woodland; general symbol

deciduous tree

evergreen tree

coniferous tree

palm

nipa palm

casuarina

filao

eucalyptus

190

Note: The small circle in the base of each of the above eight symbols only should be. included to mark the tree's location if the location is known and is of use in position fixing.

COASTLINE

inadequately surveyed coastline

steep coast

cliffy coast

sandy shore; dots on landward side

stony or **shingle shore**; texture on landward side

sandhills or **dunes**

mangrove shore

alternative to above symbol

marshy shore; where the seaward edge of the marshes is the only visible indication of the coastline, it should be indicated by a pecked line in addition to the coastline proper or the apparent coastline at high water

MARINE FEATURES AND DANGERS

danger line; dotted line encircling and emphasizing presence of danger or delimiting area containing numerous navigational dangers

swept underwater danger with depth cleared by wire drag sweep; a wreck may be marked 'Wk' (example showing depth cleared of 3.3m)

examples of **islet** or **rock** which does not cover (infilled with land tint where size permits) with elevation in metres above HW

coral reef exposed at low water (intertidal tint infill). Where coral is always covered, the symbol for underwater rock may be used.

rock exposed at low water (intertidal tint infill)

pinnacle of rock exposed at low water; alternative to above symbol

rock awash at chart datum

underwater rock lying from 0 to 20 metres

Note: A blue tint should mark rocks, wrecks, etc lying near the surface. Underwater rock(s) may be marked by the abbreviation for rock or rocky bottom (R) and a sounding figure.

stone, gravel or **shingle bottom**

191

NAUTICAL CHARTS

Note: The nature of the bottom or seabed is generally indicated by abbreviations. Where an underlying material is known to differ from the surface material, the abbreviation for the surface layer and that for the under layer should be written in that order, separated by a stroke; eg S/M = a layer of sand over mud.

mobile seabed or **sand waves**

kelp

overfalls, races and tide-rips

breakers

eddies

limit of **sea ice** (magenta, or, at junction of sea and land, black)

stranded wreck showing any portion of hull or super-structure above chart datum

alternative to above symbol – true outline of wreck infilled with intertidal tint **Wk**

dangerous wreck likely to have less than 20 metres of water over it

Note: A wreck of which the mast(s) only are visible may be marked by the above symbol with the legend 'Mast(s)' or by the dotted outline of the wreck infilled with blue and marked with the location of masts, funnels etc.

wreck in waters over 200 metres deep or in waters under 200 metres deep if the depth is unknown but the wreck is considered non-dangerous to surface vessels

unsurveyed wreck of unknown depth but considered to have a safe clearance to the depth shown **Wk**

small area of **foul ground** (such as the remains of wreck) over which it is safe to navigate but not to anchor, trawl, etc

alternative to above symbol **Foul**

alternative to above symbol for larger areas of foul ground (pecked line outline) **Foul**

offshore platform or single point mooring structure (eg for oil or gas production)

submerged wellhead (a figure for the depth may be given) **Well**

submarine pipeline; oil or gas pipe (magenta), discharge pipe (ie sewer) or cooling water intake (black)

abandoned pipeline of any type

alternative to above symbol

submarine power transmission cable

Note: Groups of pipes or cables may be indicated by marked limits to a cable or pipe area (see *Leading Lines, Tracks and Limits* below).

fishing stakes

fish trap, weir or **tunny net**

fish haven or **fishery reef** (artificial shelter of stones, concrete, scrap vehicles, etc intended to attract fish and crustaceans)

group of fish havens

LIGHTS

Note: See introductory note for character of lights.

exact **position of important light**

exact **position of minor light**

light flare (magenta or, on multicolour charts, colour to match lighter yellow for white or yellow light); used to indicate light or object with light(s) such as a lighted buoy as in the following examples:

important light

lighted buoy (example)

light vessel

lighted lanby (large automatic navigational buoy) or lighthouse buoy

floodlighting of a structure eg pier or pierhead lighthouse (magenta or, on multicolour charts, yellow)

BUOYS, BEACONS AND DAYMARKS

Note: In general, a black (ie infilled) buoy symbol implies a black buoy and an open buoy symbol implies any other colour of buoy or multicoloured buoy. Abbreviations for the colours of multicoloured buoys or beacons commence with the top colour first or, if the colours are in vertical or diagonal stripes (or if the sequence of bands is not known), the darkest colour is given first (see abbreviations in *IALA System 'A' Buoys* below).

beacon; general symbol

beacon consisting of spar or **pole placed on submerged rock** (alternative examples – topmarks as appropriate)

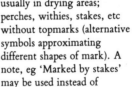

minor impermanent marks usually in drying areas; perches, withies, stakes, etc without topmarks (alternative symbols approximating different shapes of mark). A note, eg 'Marked by stakes' may be used instead of symbols.

cairn

coloured mark or white mark on cliff, rock, wall, etc; fine outline of mark with abbreviation 'Mk' (example)

noticeboard

beacon with triangular topmark

beacon consisting of painted board (possibly without pole)

NAUTICAL CHARTS

beacon tower

refuge beacon

lattice beacon

Note: A lighted beacon is generally shown by a light star and may be marked with a suitable abbreviation (eg 'Bn') if known to be a useful daymark. On large-scale charts, if appropriate, one of the above symbols may be used for a lighted beacon, with the position circle in the base replaced by a light star, eg:

lighted beacon

buoyage direction where not obvious (magenta)

conical buoy

can or **cylindrical buoy**

spherical buoy

Note: The above three symbols should not be used to indicate the float shape of pillar buoys.

pillar buoy; a buoy with a tall central structure on a broad base; in the cardinal system, most such buoys are fitted with topmarks and many with lights

spar buoy or spindle buoy without topmarks or lights

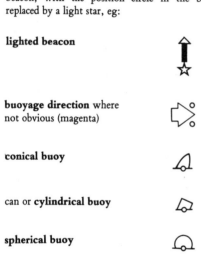

barrel buoy

light float

superbuoy, very large buoy (see *Lights* above for lanby)

mooring buoy (examples)

Note: The shape of the mooring buoy may vary but the symbol should have a ring or circle in its top. Mooring buoys with telegraphic or telephonic link should be shown with a magenta submarine cable symbol leading to them.

Note: See the following section for IALA System 'A' buoys. See *Lights* above for lighted buoys and beacons.

IALA SYSTEM 'A' BUOYS
Note: The symbols and abbreviations in this section are as used for buoys and beacons conforming to the IALA System 'A' (see introductory note). The type and significance of any buoy is indicated by the topmark (sphere, can, cone etc), colour, and character of light (if any); not by the shape of the main structure or float. Lighted buoy symbols are marked with light flare marks (see *Lights* above).

North cardinal mark buoys, black above yellow; if lighted, quick or very quick flashing white light

BY   *BY*

East cardinal mark buoys, black with single, broad, horizontal, yellow band; if lighted, three quick or very quick white flashes

BYB   *BYB*

South cardinal mark buoys, yellow above black; if lighted, six quick or very quick white flashes and one long flash

YB   *YB*

194

West cardinal mark buoys, yellow with single, broad, horizontal, black band; if lighted, nine quick or very quick white flashes

YBY   YBY

Note: The above cardinal marks have a topmark of two black cones and indicate navigable water to the named side of the mark.

port-hand lateral mark buoys, red, with red can topmark (if any); if lighted, red light, any rhythm

R   R

starboard-hand lateral mark buoys, green or black, with single green or black topmark (if any); if lighted, green light, any rhythm

B   G

Note: Lateral marks generally indicate the limits of well defined channels.

isolated-danger mark buoys (stationed over a danger with navigable water around), black with red horizontal band(s), with topmark of two black spheres; if lighted, two white flashes

BRB   BRB

safe-water mark buoys (eg mid-channel or landfall marks), red and white vertical stripes, with red sphere (if any); if lighted, white occulting, isophase or long flash

RW   RW

special mark buoys (not primarily intended for navigation but indicating special area or feature), yellow, with single yellow 'X' topmark (if any); if lighted, yellow light

Y   Y

FOG SIGNALS, RADIO AND RADAR

fog signal (magenta); symbol used in association with buoy or light symbol, or as following:

fog signal position if not closely associated with light or buoy

light with fog signal (example)

radar or radio beacon or station (small black position circle within magenta circle). The type of station or beacon may be indicated by one of the following abbreviations:

RC	non-directional (circular) radiobeacon
RD	directional radiobeacon
RW	rotating pattern radiobeacon
RG	radio direction-finding station
R	coast radio station providing QTG service
Ra	coast radar station providing range and bearing on request
Racon	radar transponder beacon – responding within the 3cm band
Racon (10cm)	radar transponder beacon – responding within the 10cm band
Ramark	radar beacon
Aero Rc	aeronautical radiobeacon

Note: Radar or radio tower, masts and scanners only of interest as visual landmarks to marine navigators are marked simply by position circles or the appropriate symbols as given in *General Structures on Land* above.

radio reporting point (calling-in or way point); vessels required to report on VHF to a traffic control centre on passing this point (magenta)

NAUTICAL CHARTS

radio reporting point
(calling-in or way point);
vessels required to report as
implied by above symbol – but
only when travelling in
direction indicated by arrow

radio reporting point with
alphanumeric designator
(example)

radar-conspicuous object

symbol used in association with beacons and
buoys fitted with radar reflectors in areas where
such devices are unusual (the symbol is not so
used where radar reflectors are commonly
fitted). The symbol may also mark natural
features known to give unexpectedly strong
radar response.

LEADING LINES, TRACKS AND LIMITS

leading line

(ie straight line passing through two or more
clearly defined, charted objects or leading
marks) should be marked by a bold continuous
line where it marks a recommended track to be
followed and by a dashed or dotted line for the
remainder of its length up to the rear mark

clearing line

(straight line marking boundary between safe
and unsafe areas or that passes clear of a
navigational danger) or transit marking isolated
dangers (marked by a fine dashed or dotted line)

example of **light
sector limits** and **arcs**
of lights that are only
visible on certain
bearings or change as
the bearings change

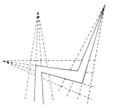

The sector limits and arcs may be indicated by
fine dashed lines or, on multicoloured charts, by
fine firm lines emphasized by colour. Sector
lines marking the edge of a fairway (sector
leading between off-lying dangers) should be
shown by fine firm lines or, on multicoloured
charts, by a yellow line overprinting the black
lines.

recommended tracks not
defined by fixed marks (one
arrow, one-way; two arrows,
two-way)

maximum draught
authorized for recommended
tracks with and without fixed
marks

recommended **deep water
track**, indicated by a dashed
line if not defined by fixed
marks (magenta)

alternative to above symbol
(magenta)

traffic separation scheme,
one-way traffic system; the
outer limits (dashed lines) may
be omitted (magenta)

roundabout in traffic
separation scheme; if no
separation zone exists, the
centre of the roundabout is
shown by a circle (magenta)

recommended direction of
traffic flow is shown by an
arrangement of dashed-outline
arrows (magenta)

limit of **restricted area**; the
downstrokes of the 'T's point
into restricted area, the nature
of the restriction being
implied by an additional
symbol or legend

fishing prohibited; symbol used with above restricted area symbol	
anchoring prohibited; symbol used with above restricted area symbol	
limit to submarine cable area; downstrokes of 'T's point into area (magenta)	
limit to submarine pipeline area; downstrokes of 'T's point into area (magenta)	
international land boundary (black)	
international maritime boundary (magenta)	
customs limit at a port (magenta)	
seaward limit of territorial seas	
fishery zone limit	
military or naval firing danger area limit (magenta)	
mine laying practice or counter-measure area limit (magenta)	
submarine exercise area or **transit lane** (magenta)	

ABBREVIATIONS

Aero	aeronautical
Al	alternating
Am	amber
B	black
bk	broken
Br	breakers
Bu	blue

C	coarse (sand)
Ca	calcareous
Cb	cobbles
CG	coastguard
Co	coral (and coralline algae)
Cup	cupola (dome)
Cy	clay
Det	detection (eg 'Fog Det Lt')
Dia	diaphone (a generally powerful, low-pitched sound, usually ending in a grunt, produced by the controlled release of compressed air)
Dir	directional (eg directional lights)
E	East
ED	existence doubtful
Explos	explosive (signal)
F	fixed (steady light)
f	fine (sand)
Fl	flashing (light)
Fla	flare
F Racon	fixed frequency racon (radar transponder beacon)
FS	flagstaff or flag pole
G	gravel
Grid	gridiron or careening grid (flat frame erected on foreshore for ships to dry out on for painting or repair at low water)
h	hard (bottom)
hor	horizontal or disposed horizontally
HW	high water
IQ	interrupted quick (flashing)
Iso	isophase (light – phased to give equal periods of light and dark)
kn	knots (ie nautical miles per hour)
LANBY	large automatic navigational buoy
Ldg	leading (lights, marks, etc)
LFl	long flash (ie a light flash of two seconds or more)
LL	list(s) of lights
Lndg	landing (eg small pier or area of hard bottom)
Lt	light
Lts	lights
LW	low water
M	sea mile (1852 metres), or mud
m	metre, or medium (sand)
Mo	morse code rhythm (light, etc)
Mon	monument

NAUTICAL CHARTS

N	North	S	sand or South
NE	North-East	s	seconds
NW	North-West	SD	doubtful sounding
		SE	South-East
Obscd	obscured	Sf	stiff
Obstn	obstruction	Sh	shells (skeletal remains)
Oc	occulting (light interrupted by regular, shorter periods of darkness)	Si	silt
		Slip	slipway
occas	occasional	so	soft
Or	orange	Sp	spire
		SPM	single point mooring structure (eg articulated tower)
P	pebbles		
PA	position approximate	SS	signal station
PD	position doubtful	St	stones
Pt	point	SW	South-West
Pyl	pylon	sy	sticky
Q	quick flashing (50 or 60 light flashes per minute)	Tr	tower
		U	unmanned
R	rock, red, or coast radio station providing 'QTG' service	v	volcanic
		vert	vertical or disposed vertically
Ra	coast radar station	Vi	violet
RC	circular (non-directional) transmission radio beacon	VQ	very quick flashing (100 or 120 light flashes per minute)
RD	directional transmission radio beacon	W	West, or white
Rep	reported	Wd	weed (including kelp, etc)
RG	radio direction finding station	Well	wellhead (oil or gas)
RoRo	roll on, roll off facility (for ferries)	Whis	whistle
Ru	ruin	Wk	wreck
RW	radio beacon with transmission in a rotating pattern	Wks	wrecks
		Y	yellow

PACKAGE AND PRODUCT LABELS

The symbols in this section may be found on products and product containers. Those marked 'ISO' conform with ISO Recommendation R 780 and have been reproduced from BS 2770:Part 1:1969. These 'ISO' markings are normally used on packaging in black or a dark colour, and with an overall size of 100, 150 or 200mm (4, 6 or 8 inches).

For labels on clothes and other fabric products see *Textiles*.

handle with care (ISO)

this way up (ISO)

centre of gravity (ISO)

sling here (ISO)

use no hooks (ISO)

keep dry (ISO)

keep away from heat (ISO)

photographic or **radiographic material** sensitive to light or other radiant energy (ie unprocessed)

PACKAGE AND PRODUCT LABELS

copyright; under the Universal Copyright Convention, the use on all copies of this symbol, together with the name of the copyright owner and the date of the first year of publication, provides copyright protection within any signatory country for works published outside its territory

the **Kitemark**, the registered trademark of the British Standards Institution. When applied to products, it implies a product has been manufactured in accordance with an appropriate British standard.

WARNING LABELS FOR HAZARDOUS SUBSTANCES

Note: The labels given below are used on containers and vehicles carrying dangerous substances and are sometimes referred to as 'hazchem' labels. The principal graphic symbol contained in each label may be found used in a different context to imply a similar warning. (For examples of this see *Signage*.)

hazardous substance (black symbol on white field); general sign used for dangerous substances for which there is no specific sign and for multi-substance loads with a variety of hazards

flammable liquid (black or white on a red field)

flammable gas (black or white on a red field)

flammable solids (black on a field of white and red vertical stripes)

dangerous when wet; warning of substances which when in contact with water emit flammable gases (black or white on a blue field)

spontaneously combustible substance (black symbol on white (upper) field with black or white letters on red (lower) field)

explosive substance (black on an orange field); sign may also contain the word 'explosive' in black letters

oxidizing substance (black on a yellow field); organic peroxides are indicated by a similar sign but with the legend 'organic peroxide' instead of 'oxidizing agent'

corrosive substance (black and white)

toxic substance (black on white); toxic gas should be indicated by a similar sign but with the legend 'toxic gas' instead of 'toxic'

harmful substance that must be kept away from food (black on white)

non-inflammable **compressed gas** (black or white on a green field)

radioactive (black and white); label used on vehicles carrying radioactive material

alternative to the above sign (black on an orange field)

radioactive; labels used on containers carrying radioactive material. The labels have one, two or three red bars (as shown) to indicate whether the contents are classified as category I, II or III.

The following symbols are used primarily in cartographic work carried out during the exploration and development of petroleum and gas deposits. The symbols may be used in conjunction with geological symbols (see *Geology*) and/or topographic symbols (see *Cartography*).

Unfortunately there is no one standard for well symbols; different geological survey departments and oil companies employ their own variations. Those given in *BMR Symbols* below form part of a range of symbols compiled, principally for geological survey work, by the staff of the Australian Bureau of Mineral Resources. The rest of the symbols in this section are taken from the *Standard Legend* produced, in 1976, by Shell Internationale Petroleum Maatschappij BV (Royal Dutch/Shell Group of Companies). This legend includes the more detailed and specific symbols required for the work of their exploration and production departments.

For engineering and piping symbols see *Engineering*.

BMR SYMBOLS

Note: Where both development and exploration wells are shown on the same map, the letter 'd' should be added to the symbols for development wells.

well – proposed site

well – drilling

well – drilling suspended

well – with show of oil, drilling suspended

well – with show of gas, drilling suspended

well – with show of gas and oil, drilling suspended

oil well

gas well

gas condensate well

well – dry, abandoned; note this symbol may be combined with any of the above six symbols to imply various abandoned wells; eg

well – with show of oil, abandoned

Note: The letters 'WI' and 'WIC' may be added to the symbol for *well – dry, abandoned* to imply **water injection well** and **control (water injection) well** respectively. The letter 'W' may be also added to any appropriate symbol to imply **water well**.

gas seep (natural)

oil seep (natural)

PRINCIPAL SYMBOLS – SHELL

location

alternative to above symbol

location proposed (large-scale maps) or **well location** (small-scale maps)

location on programme or **location approved**

drilling well (large- and small-scale maps)

drilling suspended

oil well (large- and small-scale maps)

condensate well

gas well (large- and small-scale maps)

Note: The following abbreviations may be used with the above three symbols:

F   flowing
P   pumping
GL   gas lift
PL   plunger lift
IF   intermittent flowing
IGL   intermittent gas lift
J   Jordan and Taylor
FP   'flumping'

fresh water supply

salt water supply

dry well with fresh water (small-scale maps)

dry well with salt water (small-scale maps)

exhausted well

well closed-in

well plugged and abandoned (large- and small-scale maps)

Note: The above three symbols may be used combined with the symbols for oil, gas and condensate wells; eg

exhausted gas well, plugged and abandoned

alternative symbol for **well plugged and abandoned** – for use where very small symbol is required (small-scale maps)

Note: The following abbreviations may be used adjacent to symbols for formally productive wells:

M   mechanical reasons
(P)   production method when last produced
(X-52)   date last produced
R   closed-in for repair
NC   closed-in, non-commercial
C   closed-in for conservation
GOR   closed-in for high gas oil ratio
W   closed-in for high water cut
AB   closed-in awaiting abandonment
Obs   closed-in for observation
Fac   closed-in awaiting facilities

ADDITIONAL WELL SYMBOLS – SHELL

well formally productive from deeper level, plugged back to zone of map

well formally productive from higher level, deepened to zone of map

PETROLEUM

well open to production from level higher than zone of map

zone of map had oil shows; production prospects doubtful or unknown (horizon maps)

well open to production from level lower than zone of map

zone of map had gas shows (horizon maps)

zone of map exhausted; plugged back and opened to higher level (horizon maps).

zone of map interpreted oil productive (horizon maps)

zone of map interpreted gas productive (horizon maps)

zone of map oilbearing; well open to production from level lower than zone of map (horizon maps)

zone of map interpreted gas or oil productive (horizon maps)

well producing from zone of map together with higher levels

zone of map interpreted water bearing (horizon maps)

well producing from zone of map together with lower levels

Note: The following abbreviations may be used with the above symbols:

well producing from top quarter of zone or highest of four zones represented

Ret	in returns
Ctg	in cuttings
C	in core
SWS	in sidewall samples
EL	by electric log
GR + N	by gamma ray and neutron log
TS	by temperature survey
WW	by water witch
DST	by drillstem test
PT	by production test

well producing from bottom third of zone or lowest of three zones represented

Note: In the above two symbols sectors may be shown inside or outside of the circle. The zone is shown top to bottom clockwise from the top of the circle.

zone of map missing; may be used with the following letters: sh (shaled out), f (faulted out), U (unconformity), WO (wedged out)

dual completion – both zones represented on map (higher zone represented on right of the symbol)

zone of map not reached

dual completion – lower zone only represented on map (symbol infilled on lefthand side)

gas injection well

water injection well

salt water disposal well

oil injection well

steam injection well

deviated hole (example). Surface location is indicated by small circle; infilled circle and thick line represent top of producing zone (or contour horizon) and producing interval, respectively; dotted line indicates approximate or estimated course of hole.

wells directionally drilled from one platform – no vertical hole (example)

vertical hole and wells directionally drilled from one platform (example)

This section contains symbols used in or as the emblems of political parties, movements and institutions.

Colours have long been used for party identification both to further distinguish emblems and as areas of plain colour in the form of ribbons, rosettes, backgrounds to posters and so forth. Red, with the traditional associations of blood and life, and fire and passion, has been generally accepted as the colour of revolution and used as such in the emblems of left-wing and revolutionary parties. Red has been considered and used as an auspicious colour in China since ancient times. Black generally symbolizes destruction or destructive forces (except where used in simple black and white renderings of symbols); hence the black and red flag of anarchism stands for the destruction of the old social structure and the emergence of the new. Green, with its plant-life associations, has been widely adopted by ecology parties, and, in Europe, especially West Germany, members of such parties are referred to as the 'Greens'. Green is also the colour of Ireland and therefore of Irish Republicanism. The origin of the use of other colours, such as blue by the Conservative Party (Britain), and purple and green as were used by the Suffragette Movement (Britain), is less clear.

For national emblems see *Heraldry*.

Note: Whilst every effort has been made to obtain examples of symbols used by the world's major political parties and pressure groups many political organizations are not represented in this section, because of a rather poor response to repeated attempts at obtaining examples of their symbols. The author, however, would be pleased to receive any examples of political symbols for inclusion in subsequent editions of this book.

Amnesty International

anti-nuclear power movement; usually shown with the words 'nuclear power? no thanks' in the user's language

British Movement; symbol used earlier by the National Socialist Movement (Britain) – a predecessor of the British Movement and the National Front

anarchist

Anti-Nazi League (Britain)

British Union of Fascists (now defunct)

Christelijke Volkspartij (CVP – Christian Social Party; Belgium); black on orange

Christlich Demokratische Union (CDU – Christian Democrats; Federal Republic of Germany); red capital letters, black lower case letters and a black/red/orange flag motif

Christlich Soziale Union (CSU – Christian Socialist Party; Bavarian equivalent of the CDU above); black letters with a yellow lion and a blue diamond

clenched fist; general symbol of communists, socialists and liberation movements. A version in red forms the symbol of the Socialist Workers Party (Britain).

CND (Campaign for Nuclear Disarmament)

Partito Comunista Italiano (PCI – Communist Party of Italy); red flag with yellow hammer and sickle motif superimposed on the Italian flag (green/white/red)

Conservative Party (Britain); torch symbol with blue flames and lower portion, and with red central bar

cross of Lorraine; symbol of the **Free French** forces during World War II

Democratic Party (USA); various versions of the donkey have been used to symbolize the Democratic Party in cartoons, posters, etc, but this symbol is not used as the official party logo

Democrazia Christiana (Christian Democrats Italy); red device on a white shield imposed on a blue background

dove of peace (usually with olive branch in its beak as shown); originally a religious symbol (eg the dove of Noah's Ark); now used widely by peace movements and organizations, and during celebrations of peace

the arrows and yoke symbol of the **falangists** (Spain) – see the arms of the Kingdom of Spain in *Heraldry*

fasces (Latin, literally = 'bundles'); bundle of sticks containing an axe – the symbol of justice carried by a lictor, an officer who attended the consul or dictator in Ancient Rome and carried out sentence on offenders; adopted by Mussolini as the symbol of Italian **Fascism**

POLITICS

Fine Gael (Irish Party); black on a green (top)/white/orange flag motif

gay movement

hammer and sickle; used particularly in *communist* or socialist emblems such as those of the Soviet Union and the People's Republic of China; but also used in other emblems (see *Heraldry*). Symbolizes the industrial and agricultural workers.

Labour Party (Australia)

the Australian national flag with the words 'Australian Labour Party' in blue. The Australian national flag consists of the Union Jack inset on a blue field (ie the Blue Ensign) with white stars in the form of the Southern Cross and one additional larger star (the 'Commonwealth Star') with seven points representing the six states and one territory of Australia.

Labour Party (Britain); the torch of education with a spade to represent the workers by hand and a quill pen to represent the workers by brain

Liberal Party (Australia); a blue symbol containing the Australian national flag (see *Labour Party* above)

Liberal Party (Britain)

Liberal Party (Canada); a red maple leaf

National Front (Britain); see *British Movement* above

New Democratic Party (Canada)

olive branch; ancient symbol of peace (often shown being carried by a dove – see above)

Palestine Liberation Organization

Parti Québécois (Québec, Canada)

Progressive Conservative Party (Canada); red (upper) stripe and maple leaf with a blue (lower) stripe and letters

red star, morning star; used particularly in the emblems of *communist* parties or states

Republican Party (USA); an elephant (with three white stars on a blue, upper portion divided from a red lower portion and encircling trunk by a white line)

Parti social-chrétien (PSC – Christian Socialist Party; Belgium); black and orange

Social Democratic Party (Britain); a red line beneath a blue 'S', red 'D' and blue 'P'

European **socialist**; general symbol used by various socialist parties; clenched fist grasping a red rose

Solidarity (Poland)

swastika (Hakenkreuz); symbol of the **Nazis** (German National Socialists Workers Party (NSDAP)); supposed by them to be the ancient Aryan symbol of the sun. (For other uses of this symbol – see *Religion*.) Hitler is believed to have chosen the complete form of this symbol to consist of a black swastika to represent 'the struggle for the victory of the Aryan man', a white circle behind it to represent 'the national idea' and a red background to represent 'the social idea of the movement'.

United Nations

Welsh Nationalist Party (**Plaid Cymru**); green

Women's Liberation Movement

alternative to above symbol

PROOF-READING

The following marks and conventions, extracted from BS 5261:Part 2:1976, are used widely, although variations may be found. Correction marks are used by printers, editors and authors to give instructions regarding the alteration of printers' proofs and other written material. Modern reproduction and computer techniques are changing publishing methods but, traditionally, proofs for correction have been in the form of 'galley' or 'slip' proofs consisting of printed columns of text about two feet (600 mm) long or 'page' proofs consisting of the text made up into completed pages. Any desired alteration is indicated by a mark extending through the relevant portion of the text to the margin or by two marks – one in the text at the location of the alteration and one in the margin on one or other side of the text. Where a number of instructions occur in one line, the marginal marks are divided between left and right margins where possible; the order being from left to right in both margins. If necessary, notes or the dimensions of an alteration should be given in addition to the correction mark. It is important that any marks, comments or instructions are clearly distinguishable from the copy and that the responsibility for any alteration is clearly indicated. The British standard recommends that printer's literal errors should be marked by the printer in green or by the customer and his agents in red; while other alterations and instructions by the customer and his agents should be in black or dark blue.

Note: Asterisks beside items in this section imply the following:

* where space does not permit textual marks the affected area may be encircled
** the exact dimensions should be given when necessary.

GENERAL	*Textual mark*	*Marginal mark*
Correction is concluded	none	/ after each correction
Leave unchanged	– – – – – under characters to remain	✓
Refer to appropriate authority anything of doubtful accuracy	Encircle word(s) affected.	(?)
DELETION, INSERTION AND SUBSTITUTION		
Insert in text the matter indicated in the margin	⋏	new matter followed by ⋏

	Textual mark	*Marginal mark*
Insert additional matter supplied elsewhere and identified by a letter in a diamond, eg ⬦A	⋏	⋏ followed by, eg ⬦A
Delete	/ through character or ⊢————⊣ through words to be deleted	
Delete and close up	through character or through characters; eg charaacter charaaacter	
Substitute character or substitute part of one or more word(s)	/ through character or ⊢————⊣ through word(s)	new character or new word(s)
Wrong fount; replace by character(s) of correct fount	Encircle character(s) to be changed.	⊗
Change damaged character(s) or **remove extraneous marks**	Encircle character(s) to be changed or encircle marks to be removed.	✕
Push down risen spacing material	Encircle blemish.	⊥
Set in or change to **italic**	————— under character(s) to be set or changed*	⊔

PROOF-READING

	Textual mark	Marginal mark
Set in or change to **capital letters**	≡≡≡ under character(s) to be set or changed*	≡
Set in or change to **small capital letters**	═══ under character(s) to be set or changed*	═
Set in or change to **capital letters for initial letters and small capital letters for the rest of the words**	≡≡ under initial letters and ═══ under rest of word(s)*	≡═
Set in or change to **bold type**	∿∿∿ under character(s) to be set or changed*	∿
Set in or change to **bold italic type**	∿∿∿ under character(s) to be set or changed*	⫲∿
Change **capital letters to lower case letters**	Encircle character(s) to be changed.	⧧
Change **small capital letters to lower case letters**	Encircle character(s) to be changed.	⧧
Change italic to **upright type**	Encircle character(s) to be changed.	Ψ
Invert type	Encircle character(s) to be inverted.	↺
Substitute or insert character in 'superior' position	∣ through character or ⋏ where required	Ɣ under character; eg 2Ɣ

	Textual mark	*Marginal mark*
Substitute or insert character in 'inferior' position	**/** through character or **ʎ** where required	ʆ over character; eg ʆ₂
Substitute **ligature** eg ffi for separate letters	⊢────┤ through characters affected	‿ eg ffi
Substitute **separate letters** for ligature	⊢────┤	Write out separate letters.
Substitute or insert **full stop** or decimal point	**/** through character or **ʎ** where required	⊙
Substitute or insert **colon**	**/** through character or **ʎ** where required	⊙
Substitute or insert **semi-colon**	**/** through character or **ʎ** where required	;
Substitute or insert **comma**	**/** through character or **ʎ** where required	,

PROOF-READING

	Textual mark	Marginal mark
Substitute or insert **apostrophe**	**/** through character or **ʌ** where required	ᕣ
Substitute or insert **single quotation marks**	**/** through character or **ʌ** where required	ᕤ and/or ᕣ
Substitute or insert **double quotation marks**	**/** through character or **ʌ** where required	ᕤᕤ and/or ᕣᕣ
Substitute or insert **ellipsis**	**/** through character or **ʌ** where required	. . .
Substitute or insert **leader dots**	**/** through character or **ʌ** where required	⊙⋯⊙ The measure of the leader should be given when necessary.
Substitute or insert **hyphen**	**/** through character or **ʌ** where required	⊢⊣

	Textual mark	*Marginal mark*
Substitute or insert **rule**	/ through character or ⅄ where required	⊢⊣ The size of the rule should be given; eg ⊢1 em⊣ ⊢4mm⊣
Substitute or insert **oblique**	/ through character or ⅄ where required	⊘

POSITIONING AND SPACING		
Start new paragraph		
Run on (no new paragraph)		
Transpose characters or words	between characters or words, numbered when necessary	
Transpose a number of characters or words	3 2 1 | | | The vertical strokes are made through the characters or words to be transposed and numbered in the correct sequence.	1 2 3
Transpose lines		

PROOF-READING

	Textual mark	*Marginal mark*
Transpose a number of lines	——— 3 ——— 2 ——— 1 Rules extend from the margin into the text with each line to be transplanted numbered in the correct sequence.	
Centre	⌈enclosing matter⌉ ⌊to be centred ⌋	[ ]
Indent		The amount of the indent should be given.
Cancel indent		
Set line justified to specified measure	⊢[and/or]⊣	⊢⊣ **
Set column justified to specified measure	⊢——⊣	⊢⊣ **
Move matter specified distance to the right	⌈enclosing matter to ⌉ ⌊be moved to the right⌋	**
Move matter specified distance to the left	⊢⌈enclosing matter to ⌉ ⌊be moved to the left⌋	**
Take over character(s), word(s) or line to next line, column or page	The textual mark surrounds the matter to be taken over and extends into the margin.	

	Textual mark	Marginal mark
Take back character(s), word(s), or line to previous line, column or page		The textual mark surrounds the matter to be taken back and extends into the margin.
Raise matter	over matter to be raised under matter to be raised	**
Lower matter	over matter to be lowered under matter to be lowered	**
Move matter to position indicated	Enclose matter to be moved and indicate new position.	**
Correct vertical alignment		
Correct horizontal alignment	single line above and below misaligned matter eg mi$_s$a^{l}i^{g}n$_e$d	The marginal mark is placed level with the head and foot of the relevant line.
Close up; delete space between characters or words	eg linking characters	
Insert space between characters	between characters affected	**
Insert space between words	between words affected	**

PROOF-READING

	Textual mark	*Marginal mark*
Reduce space between characters	| between characters affected	⌒ **
Reduce space between words	⌒ between words affected	⌒ **
Make space appear equal between characters or words	| between characters or words affected	⫩
Close up to normal interline spacing	(each side of column linking lines)	The textual marks extend ** into the margin.
Insert space between lines or paragraphs	or	The marginal mark extends ** between the lines of text.
Reduce space between lines or paragraphs	or	The marginal mark extends ** between the lines of text.

Punctuation is here considered in its broadest sense: this section contains symbols and conventions used to enhance the meaning, form and sound of written English, by indicating stops, pauses, gaps, links, emphasis and accent.

There is much dispute as to the correct use of many of these symbols; explanations given below refer to widely accepted practice. However, many creative writers have legitimately used unusual punctuation to improve the effectiveness of their work (classic examples of this may be found in the works of Lawrence Sterne). Good advice on the use of punctuation is given in *The Complete Plain Words* (Gowers/rev. Fraser): 'Taste and common sense are more important than any rules; you put in stops to help your reader to understand you, not to please grammarians. And you should try so to write that he will understand you with the minimum of help of that sort.'

See *Proof Reading* for marks used in text and print correction. See *Mathematics* for the mathematic usage of symbols for full stop, exclamation mark, brackets, braces, dash and accent.

a **paragraph** is normally indicated by its first word being written on a new line of the text and set in from the lefthand margin (indented). However, it may be indicated without indentation but with an enlarged gap between the last line of one paragraph and the first of the next. The commencement of a new paragraph implies a substantial pause, allowing the reader time for thought and breath, and divides the writing into convenient subject-sections for reference and comprehension.

paragraph; normally used as an alternative to above paragraph conventions or to stress them, or as a symbol for the word 'paragraph'　　¶

general alternative to the above symbol, meaning **paragraph, section** or **division**　　§

comma; implies a pause or separation slightly greater than that which exists simply between words. It is used where such a pause clarifies the meaning of a sentence; such as between words or statements forming a list or series, or to indicate parenthesis; eg The Bishop's dog, which I detested, had died.　　,

semi-colon; implies a greater pause or separation between words than does a comma but a lesser break than does a full stop. It is used to imply a pause between two linked or contrasted statements not connected by a conjunction such as 'and'; eg The adult eagle is very attractive; its young are ugly. It is also used to divide up a sentence into major sections when minor divisions are indicated by commas.　　;

colon; implies a greater pause or division than does a semi-colon and therefore may be used to indicate a major division in a sentence containing minor divisions indicated by semi-colons and commas, or to mark more strongly than would a semi-colon the contrast between two statements. It is also used to imply a pause between a word or statement and further details; eg The bakery uses many types of flour: rye and maize flours, and a variety of wheat-flour grades.　　:

PUNCTUATION

full stop or period; primarily implies the pause and break in continuity at the end of a sentence or unit of thought. The symbol also can be used to indicate the omission of letters in an **abbreviation** (eg U.N., Staffs.), although many contractions are commonly used without dots (eg tan, sin, BBC).

.

exclamation mark; used in the place of a full stop at the end of exclamatory sentences, or used after particular exclamatory word(s) within a sentence; eg Hark! the wind whistles through the trees.

!

question mark or interrogation point; used after a direct question, normally at the end of a sentence where it replaces the full stop, although it also may be used after a question within a sentence; eg Do you know the value of this painting? or its importance to the collection?

?

ellipsis, (normally) three dots; indicates an omission of words (particularly in quotations) or hesitant, broken or unfinished sentences. If the omission is of the end of a sentence a full-stop ellipsis (four dots) may be used; eg The door slowly opened and . . . .

. . .

brackets; used to enclose word(s) or letter(s) to indicate parenthesis, ie that the enclosed matter is an aside or a non-essential addition to the main meaning.

( )

square brackets; alternative to above symbol; commonly used, in preference to the above symbol, to enclose matter written by someone other than the author of the main body of a written passage (eg an editor). Also may be used to enclose word groups which include words enclosed by the above brackets.

[ ]

braces; alternative to the above two symbols; normally used to enclose more than one line of text

{ }

dash; used between words to imply a pause and, often, to suggest dramatic emphasis prior to a conclusion, or something unexpected or of special importance. Also sometimes used before and after a word or group of words to indicate parenthesis, in a similar manner to brackets; eg The animal – born without teeth – crushed its prey.

—

hyphen; used to link words to form compound words (eg forget-me-not) and to maintain meaning (eg deep-sea fishing). Also used to link but keep separate certain prefixes and root words (eg by-product, in-law) and to prevent a lower-case letter and a capital letter, two identical vowels or three identical consonants from being run together in a compound word (eg anti-Russian, co-operate, grass-seed).

-

apostrophe; used to indicate the omission of letters in a word (eg it's = it is), the possessive of nouns (eg Tom's bat) or to denote plurals of symbols, letters, numbers and words as words (eg The r's in all the Rome's are in the wrong typeface). An apostrophe is not used in possessive pronouns (ie its, hers, ours, yours, theirs) except for 'one's'. Opinion varies as to the correct form of the possessive of words ending in 's'; those of one syllable may be given a second 's' (eg Davy Jones's locker) while usually only an apostrophe is added to those of more than one syllable (eg Phyllis' book). The apostrophe is used in the normal form of certain names (eg D'Arcy, O'Connor).

'

quotation marks; inverted commas placed before and after words or groups of words primarily imply the enclosed words are reported speech (eg He said, "Go home!") or a direct literary quotation or title. Where a quotation extends over several paragraphs, quotation marks are normally used at the beginning of each paragraph and at the end of the final paragraph. They also may be used on either side of particular words to differentiate them from the rest of a text; particularly to imply that they are slang or technical jargon.

" "

quotation marks; alternative to the above symbol. If one symbol form is generally used to enclose quotations, the other form may be used to enclose a quotation within a quotation; eg She replied, 'I heard him say, "Go home!" '

' '

italics (example); a form of sloping type chiefly used in printed matter to make particular words distinct from the remainder of the text or to give them emphasis

juggle

capital letters (examples); generally used for the first letter of sentences, lines of poetry and proper nouns (including words for personified objects or qualities; eg 'my friend, Death'); and are used for the pronoun 'I' and the vocative 'O'. Adjectives derived from proper nouns normally retain a capital (eg Germany – German). Only the important words of multi-word names, such as the titles of books and the names of certain places, are normally given capital initial letters (eg Bridge of Orchy, the College of Arms).

ABCD

Note: 'Use a capital for the particular and a small letter for the general' – advice given in *The Complete Plain Words* (see introductory note above).

asterisk; an item and a reference to it elsewhere may be visually linked by both being marked with one or the same number of asterisks. Also, occasionally, used to indicate the omission of certain letters or words.

*

dagger; alternative to above symbol, used to indicate footnotes

†

double dagger; alternative to above symbol

‡

diaeresis; two dots over the second of two vowels implies that they should be pronounced separately (eg creätive = cre-ative)

¨

accent; (if used) is usually placed after the accented syllable in an English word (eg enam' el, mishap')

'

short vowel; may be used over a short vowel (eg răck) or vowels (eg tŏok)

˘

long vowel; may be used over a long vowel (eg tāke) or vowels (eg mōon)

¯

Note: The above four symbols are rarely used except in explanations of pronunciation, such as are to be found in dictionaries.

RELIGION

The symbols in this section may be found in religious illustrations and decorations in books and pictures and on buildings and monuments. See *Heraldry* for Christian symbolic meanings for creatures and plants, ecclesiastical insignia, and for additional representations of the Cross.

Note: The Cross, symbolizing Jesus Christ's crucifixion and the redeeming benefits of his passion and death, is therefore also the sign of Christ and of the Christian faith in general.

Latin cross

Greek cross

St Andrew's cross

Celtic cross

chi-rho monogram; the first two letters of 'ΧΡΙΣΤΟΣ' ('CHRIST' in Greek) in the form of a cross

alternative to above symbol

ankh; symbol of life of the Ancient Egyptians; used widely as a cross-form on Coptic Christian monuments

swastika (name probably from Sanskrit, *svasti* 'well-being')

Jaina cross, Buddhist cross, gammadion (ie cross formed from four Greek capitals of the letter gamma); a widely used ancient symbol of good fortune, today particularly used by Jains as an auspicious symbol connected with the seventh Jina. Used on certain early Christian tombs as a veiled reference to the Cross.

the **T'ai Chi** (supreme ultimate)

diagram expressing the complementary duality or action and reaction of *Yin and Yang* that produces, maintains and exists in all things; a central concept and symbol in Taoism. Yin (literally 'dark side' of a hill) is the dark, negative, female, rest principle. Yang (literally 'light side' of a hill) is the light, positive, male, action and aggression principle. Each half of the diagram may contain a dot of its opposite colour (ie a black dot on the Yang side and a white dot on the Yin side, as shown here) to represent the seed of its opposite existing within each quality.

Yin (see above); used with following symbol, particularly in *I Ching* divination

Yang (see above)

the **Wheel of Life**, the Wheel of Becoming

Buddhist and Jain symbol representing endless life from birth to rebirth; may be decorated to depict the nature of human progress and suffering through life. In Buddhism, the symbol with eight spokes may also be considered as representing the Noble Eightfold Path (right understanding, right intention, right speech, right conduct, right occupation, right exertion, right contemplation or mind control, right meditation) which may enable one to attain Nirvana and thus leave the Wheel of Life.

Note: The *circle* is a universal symbol of totality, eternity and eternal cyclic processes, and, therefore, may also represent God or the self. The heavens may be represented by a circle in Chinese symbolism. In Zen Buddhism, an empty circle may imply enlightenment. Halos, usually depicted as circle(s) or a disk, with or without rays, encircling a person's head or entire body, have been widely used since ancient times to imply radiant holiness or spiritual power.

the **Seal of Solomon**, the Mogun David, Shield or Star of David

a symbol of Judaism. Also used as a charm giving spirit power over matter and supernatural beings such as genii. The interlaced triangles have been considered as depicting the perfect balance or union of all elements or forces of a celestial nature (represented by the upright triangle) with those of an opposite, terrestrial nature (represented by the inverted triangle); male and female, fire and water, white and black and so on.

crescent

first used on the standard of the infantry of the Ottoman Turks under Sultan Orkhan (1326-60) and came to be generally used on Islamic military standards, national flags and on the tops of minarets and other religious monuments, often together with a star, to indicate sovereignty or divinity. Also used in the symbol of the Red Crescent (the Islamic equivalent to the Red Cross).

ROMAN NUMERALS

The Roman numerals for numbers between one and ten are similar to the Etruscan numerals I (1), II (2), III (3), IIII (4), ∧(5) and X (10), and may have been adapted from them. Originally the V may have been a pictorial representation of an open hand with its five fingers. The X was probably formed from two Vs.

For the units for 50, 100 and 1000, the Romans appear to have adapted the Greek letters of chi, theta and phi; chi (in classical times, sometimes written as ⊥ or ↓ becoming L, theta (θ) becoming C, which is also an abbreviation for centum (hundred), and phi(ϕ) becoming I or M – M also being an abbreviation for mille (thousand). For numbers of 1000 and more, various methods and symbols were used. One method used in the Middle Ages, that of marking a bar over a numeral (see below), does not appear to have been used in classical times; although a similarly placed bar was sometimes employed to distinguish numerals from nouns.

The subtractive system (IV instead of IIII for 4, XL instead of XXXX for 40, etc), which is now the normal practice, was rarely used until comparatively recent times.

1	I	30	XXX
2	II	40	XL
3	III	50	L
4	IV	60	LX
alternative to above symbol; the form used on clock and watch faces	IIII	70	LXX
		80	LXXX
		90	XC
5	V	100	C
6	VI	200	CC
7	VII	300	CCC
8	VIII	400	CD
9	IX	alternative to above symbol	CCCC
10	X	500	D
11	XI	alternative to above symbol	IↃ
12	XII	800	DCCC
13	XIII	alternative to above symbol	IↃↃↃ
14	XIV	900	CM
15	XV	alternative to above symbol	DCCCC
16	XVI	1000	M
17	XVII	alternative to above symbol	CIↃ
18	XVIII	1983	MCMLXXXIII
19	XIX	2000	MM
20	XX	3000	MMM
21	XXI		
22	XXII	Note: Roman numerals higher than those given above are rarely encountered in modern usage.	
23	XXIII		
24	XXIV	10,000	CCIↃↃ
25	XXV	100,000	CCCIↃↃↃ
26	XXVI	1,000,000	CCCCIↃↃↃↃ

ROMAN NUMERALS

Note: An example of an early form of the above method of denoting 1000s is to be found on the Columna Rostrata (a monument, to the victory in 260 BC over the Carthaginians, erected in the Roman forum) where the number 2,300,000 is represented by a form of the symbol CCCIƆƆ repeated 23 times.

1000	$\bar{\text{I}}$
10,000	$\bar{\text{X}}$
100,000	$\bar{\text{C}}$

Note: In the above system, which was employed in the Middle Ages, the bar (vinculum, titulus)

placed over a figure implies that it is multiplied by 1000.

1000,000 (used in the Middle Ages)	$	\overline{\text{X}}	$
alternative to above symbol (used in the Middle Ages)	$	\text{X}	$
100,000,000 (used in the Middle Ages)	$	\overline{\text{M}}	$
three alternatives for 1000 used in the past but no longer in use	⓪
	∞
	∝

Graphic symbols are today widely used in safety and information signs, especially in industry and transport.

The examples of safety signs given in this section conform to those given in BS 5378: Part 1:1980 which was prepared with due regard to the work that had been completed on international safety signs. The relevant international standard, ISO 3864, has yet to be published.

Apart from the 'handicapped' sign which is well established internationally, information signs vary greatly between countries and organizations, although the variations are more in style than content. The examples given here are used in airports owned and operated by the British Airports Authority.

For signs used on containers and vehicles carrying hazardous substances see *Package and Product Labels*. See also *Highway Signs*.

SAFETY SIGNS

Note: Signs other than those given in this section may be employed. If conforming to BS 5378, these should have a similar format and colours to those given here: signs implying 'stop' or a prohibition consisting of a black symbol on a white background within a red circle with a red diagonal band; warning signs consisting of a black symbol on a yellow triangle with a black surround; signs requiring mandatory action consisting of a white symbol or text on a blue background; signs implying safe conditions, safety or rescue equipment, escape routes and so forth having a green background. It is usual for fire-fighting equipment to be red or marked with red.

pedestrians prohibited (black symbol on a white field, with red circle and bar)

not drinking water (black symbols on a white field, with red circle and bar)

do not extinguish with water (black symbols on a white field, with red circle and bar)

no smoking (black symbol on a white field, with red circle and bar)

smoking and naked flames prohibited (black symbol on a white field, with red circle and bar)

caution – risk of fire (yellow and black)

caution – risk of explosion (yellow and black)

caution – toxic hazard (yellow and black)

danger identification (black and yellow or fluorescent orange-red); sign used to mark the perimeter of a hazard

caution – corrosive substance (yellow and black)

eye protection must be worn (blue and white)

caution – risk of ionizing radiation (yellow and black)

hearing protection must be worn (blue and white)

caution – risk of electrical shock (yellow and black)

respiratory protection must be worn (blue and white)

caution – laser beam (yellow and black)

head protection must be worn (blue and white)

caution – overhead load (yellow and black)

foot protection must be worn (blue and white)

caution – industrial trucks (yellow and black)

hand protection must be worn (blue and white)

caution – danger (yellow and black); general warning sign

SIGNAGE

first aid (green and white)

nursing mothers' room, nursery

INFORMATION SIGNS
Note: Alternatives to the following signs may be encountered – see introduction.

male, men, men's toilet facility

first aid

female, women, women's toilet facility

telephone

Note: The abbreviation 'WC' (water closet) can be used for indicating toilet facilities.

facility for the **handicapped**

post office, postal facilities

banking, exchange facilities

shower facility

information, enquiries

drinking water

buffet, tea or coffee

bar

restaurant, eating facility

left-luggage facility

luggage reclaim

lift, elevator

taxis, taxi rank

car hire

buses, bus or coach station

trains, railway station

airport arrivals and
departures, airport

helicopters, heliport

In recent years an attempt has been made to establish an international range of symbols to be used on care labels on garments and other textile products. Except where stated otherwise, the following symbols conform with BS 2747:1980 and, with certain local variations, are in general use in Europe. In the USA, a brief written description of care and washing requirements is normally given on each textile label.

Note: The following symbols generally imply processes approved for the care of an article by its manufacturer.

machine-wash (example);

the figure below the 'wave' line gives the temperature (in degrees Centigrade) for the wash, the figure above the 'wave' line indicates the type of wash required. The meaning of this second number varies; in many countries, the requirements for mechanical action (machine agitation) are described as 'normal', 'reduced' and 'much reduced' instead of 'maximum', 'medium' and 'minimum' as below. The meanings given for the following numbers are those used in Britain (to accord with BS 2747: 1980).

1   maximum temperature – 95°C
    mechanical action – maximum
    rinsing – normal
    spinning or wringing – normal

2   maximum temperature – 60°C
    mechanical action, rinsing and water
    extraction as 1

3   maximum temperature – 60°C
    mechanical action – medium
    rinsing with gradual cooling before spinning
    reduced spinning or wringing at reduced
    pressure

4   maximum temperature – 50°C
    mechanical action, rinsing and water
    extraction as 3

5   maximum temperature – 40°C
    mechanical action – maximum
    rinsing with gradual cooling before spinning
    reduced spinning or wringing at reduced
    pressure

6   maximum temperature – 40°C
    mechanical action – medium
    rinsing and water extraction as 5

7   maximum temperature – 40°C
    mechanical action – minimum
    rinsing – normal
    spinning or machine wringing – normal
    do not wring by hand

8   maximum temperature – 30°C
    mechanical action – minimum
    rinsing – normal
    reduced spinning or wringing at reduced
    pressure

9   maximum temperature – 95°C
    mechanical action – minimum
    drip dry

hand-wash (with a short wash time) at a maximum temperature of 40°C, rinse and gently squeeze by hand. Do not wring. Do not machine wash

a bar beneath a 'wash-tub' symbol (as in this example) implies **reduced mechanical treatment**; this international convention does not form part of BS 2747:1980

chlorine-based bleaching processes may be used

cool iron at a maximum temperature of 110°C

warm iron at a maximum temperature of 150°C

hot iron at a maximum temperature of 200°C

dry clean normally, in any solvents normally used for dry cleaning

dry clean normally, in certain solvents; viz tetrachloroethylene, trichlorofluoromethane (solvent 11), hydrocarbons (white spirit), trichlorotrifluoroethane (solvent 113) using any normal dry cleaning processes

dry clean using certain methods and solvents; ie hydrocarbons (white spirit), trichlorotrifluoroethane (solvent 113), tetrachloroethylene and trichlorofluoromethane (solvent 11) may be used but only in certain specific processes and with a very strict limitation on the addition of water during cleaning

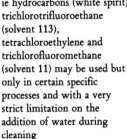

dry clean normally, in limited solvents; viz hydrocarbons (white spirits) and trichlorofluoroethane

dry clean using limited methods and solvents; ie hydrocarbons (white spirit), and trichlorotrifluoroethane may be used but only in certain specific processes and with a very strict limitation on the addition of water during cleaning

tumble dry

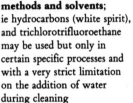

Note: In 1982, the technical committee of **GINETEX** (the International Association for Textile Care Labelling) recommended that the circle in the above symbol should contain one or two dots; one dot to imply 'gentle tumbler-drying of the textile at a lower thermal level (max 60°C)', and two dots to imply 'tumbler-drying without restriction is possible'.

do not; a cross superimposed on any one of the above symbols implies that the process should not be carried out; eg

do not iron

The modern international metric system of units of measurement, known as SI (the International System or Le Système International d'Unités), has largely replaced the earlier CGS System (based on the units of the centimetre, gram — or gramme, and second); however, CGS units may still be encountered in countries and fields of activity where there has been a tradition of their use. The SI base units are the metre, kilogram, second, ampere, kelvin, mole and candela. In addition to these, there are two units, known as SI supplementary units; the geometrical units of the radian and the steradian. All other SI units may be expressed in terms of one or more of these nine units and are therefore known as SI derived units. A number of these SI derived units, such as the newton (N), have their own special names and symbols, while others are represented by algebraic expressions composed of SI base and supplementary units; for instance, the candela per square metre (cd/m^2). As these algebraic expressions are generally self-explanatory, only a selection of these is given below.

Prefixes may be added to SI symbols and names to imply decimal multiples and sub-multiples of units; eg km (kilometre) = 1000 m (thousand metres), μs (microsecond) = 0.000 001 s (millionth of a second). As, for historical reasons, the base unit of mass is the kilogram (1000 grams), masses are expressed as multiples and sub-multiples of the gram; eg $\mu g = 10^{-9}kg$. In the case of any symbol with a prefix and an exponent, the exponent implies that the multiple or sub-multiple of the unit is raised to the power indicated; for instance, $1 \, cm^2 = 10^{-4}m^2$ or the area of a square with sides of 1 cm; thus 10,000 cm^2 = 1 m^2.

The body today responsible for the development and maintenance of the International System of Units, the International Bureau of Weights and Measures (BIPM), was set up by the Metre Convention signed in Paris by 17 countries on 20 May 1875. (Today the membership of this convention includes the following countries: Argentina, Australia, Austria, Belgium, Brazil, Bulgaria, Cameroon, Canada, Chile, Czechoslovakia, Denmark, Dominican Republic, Egypt, Federal Republic of Germany, Finland, France, German Democratic Republic, Hungary, India, Indonesia, Iran, Ireland, Italy, Japan, Korea, Mexico, the Netherlands, Norway, Pakistan, Poland, Portugal, Rumania, Spain, South Africa, Sweden, Switzerland, Thailand, Turkey, Uruguay, UK, USA, USSR, Venezuela, Yugoslavia.)

The work of the BIPM is supervised by the CIPM (the International Committee of Weights and Measures) under the authority of CGPM (General Conference of Weights and Measures — the meeting of representatives of all member states of the Metre Convention).

Prior to the development of the metric system, various *traditional units* of measurement were employed. Of these traditional units, only the units of time, the second (s), minute (min), hour (h), and day (d), remain in use with units of the International System. However, refined versions of traditional units belonging to what is sometimes referred to as the Fps System (a system of units based on the foot, pound and second), continue to be widely used for non-scientific purposes in certain countries; in particular the United States. The principal traditional units of length, area, volume and mass are as follows:

length – inch, foot (12 in), yard (3 ft), mile (1760), pole (5½ yd), chain (22 yd), furlong (220 yd), fathom (unit used for nautical lengths and depths, 1 fathom = 6 ft)

area or square measure – square inch, square foot (144 sq in), square yard (9 sq ft), acre (4840 sq yd), square mile (640 acres), perch (30¼ sq yd), rood (40 perches)

volume or capacity – fluid ounce, pint (1 pt (UK) = 20 fl oz (UK); 1 pt (US) = 16 fl oz (US)), quart (2 pt), gallon (4 qt), peck (2 gal), bushel (8 gal), quarter (8 bushels), barrel (dry barrel (US) = 7056 in^3 (115.627 dm^3); (petroleum) barrel (US) = 9702 in^3 (158.987 dm^3)). Volume may be also indicated by using the cubic inch, cubic foot, cubic yarding, etc.

mass or weight (avoirdupois weight) – grain (1/7000 lb), dram (27.34 gr), ounce (16 drams), pound (16 oz), stone (14 lb), quarter (2 st), hundredweight (4 qr), ton (20 cwt)

INTERNATIONAL UNITS

Note: This section contains symbols for SI base units (marked *), SI derived units (marked **), SI supplementary units (marked ***), and other units which, although not part of the International System, may be used with SI units.

degree (plane angle); 360th of a circle; see also °C below   °

minute (plane angle); 60th of a degree   ′

second (plane angle); 60th of a minute   ′ ′

gamma (magnetic flux density); $1\gamma = 10^{-9}$ T; use of this unit not recommended by CIPM, γ may also be used to imply 10^{-9} kg (this practice also not recommended by CIPM) γ

micron (length); $1\mu = 10^{-6}$ m = 1μm; use of this symbol not recommended by CIPM μ

ohm** (electrical resistance); $1\Omega = 1V/A = 1\ m^2 \cdot kg \cdot s^{-3} \cdot A^{-2}$ Ω

ampere* (electric current); 'The ampere is that constant current which, if maintained in two straight parallel conductors of infinite length, of negligible circular cross-section, and placed 1 metre apart in vacuum, would produce between these conductors a force equal to 2×10^{-7} newton per metre of length.' (CIPM, Resolution 2, 1946 – approved by CGPM, 1948)   A

are (area); 1a = 100m^2 a

ångström (length); 1Å = 10^{-10}m   Å

German alternative to AU   AE

Russian alternative to AU   a.e.Д

ampere per metre** (magnetic field strength)   A/m

ampere per square metre** current density)   A/m^2

standard atmosphere (pressure); 1 atm = 101325 Pa   atm

astronomical unit (distance); 1 AU = 149597870 km; *see Astronomy*   AU

UNITS OF MEASUREMENT

barn (area — unit used in measurements of cross-sections of nuclei); 1 b $= 10^{-28} m^2$ — b

bar (pressure); 1 bar $= 10^5$ Pa — bar

becquerel** (radioactive activity); 1 Bq $= 1 s^{-1}$ — Bq

coulomb** (quantity [charge] of electricity); 1C $= 1 s \cdot A$ — C

degree Celsius** (temperature); the original Celsius or centigrade scale of temperature was defined by 0 being the melting point of water and 100 being the boiling point of water. This has been considered insufficiently precise for scientific purposes and therefore the present Celsius scale has been redefined so that 1 unit C = 1 unit K, and 0 C = 273.15 K. — °C

candela* (luminous intensity); 'The candela is the luminous intensity, in the perpendicular direction, of a surface of 1/600 000 square metre of a black body at the temperature of freezing platinium under a pressure of 101325 newton per square metre.' (13th CGPM, 1967, Resolution 5) — cd

candela per square metre** (luminance) — cd/m^2

curie (activity of a radioactive substance); 1 Ci $= 3.7 \times 10^{10}$Bq — Ci

day (time); 1 d $= 24$ h $= 86\ 400$ s — d

dyne (force); 1 dyn $= 10^{-5}$N; CGS unit not recommended for use with SI units by CIPM — dyn

erg (energy); 1 erg $= 10^{-7}$J; CGS unit not recommended for use with SI units by CIPM — erg

electron volt (energy — unit used in nuclear physics); 1 eV = the kinetic energy acquired by an electron when passing through a potential difference of 1 volt in vacuum $= 1.60219 \times 10^{-19}$J approximately — eV

farad** (capacitance); 1F $= 1$ C/V $= 1m^{-2} \cdot kg^{-1} \cdot s^4 \cdot A^2$ — F

gauss (magnetic flux density); 1G corresponds but is not strictly equal to 10^{-4}T in SI units; CGS unit not recommended for use with SI units by CIPM — G

gram (mass); 1g $= 10^{-3}$kg (see *prefixes* in introduction to this section). Alternatively this symbol may be used for **grade** or **gon** (plane angle); 1 grade $= \pi/200$ rad. — g

gal (acceleration due to gravity — unit used in geodesy); 1 Gal $= 1$ cm/s^2; for gallon see *Traditional Units* below — Gal

alternative to G, above — Gs

gray** (absorbed dose of ionizing radiation); 1Gy $= 1$J/kg $= 1m^2 \cdot s^{-2}$ — Gy

henry** (inductance); 1H $= 1$Wb/A $= 1m^2 \cdot kg \cdot s^{-2} \cdot A^{-2}$ — H

hour (time); 1h $= 60$ min $= 3600$s — h

hectare (acre); 1 ha $= 10^4 m^2$ — ha

henry per metre** (permeability) — H/m

hertz** (frequency); 1Hz $= 1s^{-1}$ — Hz

joule** (energy); 1J $= 1$N $\cdot$ m $= 1m^2 \cdot kg \cdot s^{-2}$ — J

kelvin* (thermodynamic temperature); 'The kelvin, unit of thermodynamic temperature, is the fraction 1/273.16 of the thermodynamic temperature of the triple point of water.' (13th CGPM, 1967, Resolution 4) — K

kilogram* (mass); the kilogram is a mass equal to the international kilogram prototype (a platinum-iridium cylinder kept at the BIPM) — kg

kilogram-force (force); 1kgf = 9.80665N; use of this unit not recommended by CIPM — kgf

kilogram per cubic metre** (density) — kg/m^{-3}

litre (volume); 1l = 1dm³; use of this unit not recommended by CIPM for high accuracy measurements — l

lumen** (luminous flux); 1lm = 1cd·sr — lm

alternative to l — ltr

lux** (illuminance); $1lx = 1lm/m^2 = 1m^{-2}·cd·sr$ — lx

(international) **nautical mile** (distance); 1M = 1852m; the British nautical mile (no longer used by the British Admiralty) = 6080 feet — M

metre* (length); 'The metre is the length equal to 1650763.73 wavelengths in vacuum of the radiation corresponding to the transition between the levels $2p_{10}$ and $5d_5$ of the krypton-86 atom' (11th CGPM, 1960, Resolution 6) — m

1 per metre** (wave number) — m^{-1}

square metre** (area) — m^2

cubic metre** (volume) — m^3

minute (time); 1min = 60s — min

cubic metre per kilogram** (specific volume) — m^3/kg

mole (amount of substance); 'The mole is the amount of substance of a system which contains as many elementary entities as there are atoms in 0·012 kilogram of carbon 12' (definition adopted by 14th CGPM, 1971). When a mole is used, the elementary units (such as molecules, atoms or electrons) under consideration must be specified. — mol

mole per cubic metre** (concentration of amount of substance) — mol/m^3

maxwell (magnetic flux); 1Mx corresponds to, but is not strictly equal to, 10^{-8}Wb; CGS unit not recommended for use with SI units by CIPM — Mx

newton** (force); $1N = 1m·kg·s^{-2}$ — N

oersted (magnetic field strength, magnetic intensity); 1Oe corresponds to, but is not strictly equal to, $(1000/4\pi)$ A/m; CGS unit not recommended for use with SI units by CIPM — Oe

poise (viscosity); $1P = 1dyn·s/cm^2 = 0.1Pa·s$; CGS unit not recommended for use with SI units by CIPM — P

pascal** (pressure, stress); $1Pa = 1N/m^{-2} = 1m^{-1}·kg·s^{-2}$ — Pa

parsec (distance); 1 pc = 206265 AU see *Astronomy* — pc

phot (illumination); $1ph = 10^4 1x$; CGS unit not recommended for use with SI units by CIPM — ph

röntgen (exposure of X or μ radiation); $1R = 2.58 \times 10^{-4}$C/kg — R

UNITS OF MEASUREMENT

radian* (plane angle); '1 rad is the angle between two radii of a circle which cut off on the circumference an arc equal in length to the radius' (ISO standard 31/1, 1978). Alternatively this symbol may be used for **rad** (see below). — rad

rad (absorbed dose of ionizing radiations); $1 \text{ rd} = 10^{-2}\text{Gy}$ — rd

siemens** (electrical conductance); $1 \text{ S} = 1 \text{ A/V} = 1 \text{ m}^{-2}\cdot\text{kg}^{-1}\cdot\text{s}^3\cdot\text{A}^2$ — S

second* (time); 'The second is the duration of 9 192 631 770 periods of the radiation corresponding between the two hyperfine levels of the ground state of the caesium-133 atom.' (13th CGPM, Resolution 1) — s

stilb (luminance); $1\text{sb} = 10^4\text{cd/m}$; CGS unit not recommended for use with SI units by CIPM — sb

steradian* (solid angle); '1sr is the solid angle which, having its vertex in the centre of a sphere, cuts off an area of the surface of the sphere equal to that of a square with sides of length equal to the radius of the sphere.' (ISO standard 31/1, 1978) — sr

stoke (kinematic viscosity); $1\text{St} = 1\text{cm}^2/\text{s}$; CGS unit not recommended for use with SI units by CIPM — St

stere (volume — unit used in measurements of firewood); $1\text{st} = 1\text{m}^3$; use of this unit not recommended by CIPM — st

tesla** (magnetic flux density); $1\text{T} = 1\text{Wb/m}^2 = 1\text{kg}\cdot\text{s}^{-2}\cdot\text{A}^{-1}$ — T

tonne (mass); $1\text{t} = 10^3\text{kg}$ — t

unified atomic mass unit (mass – unit used for expressing the masses of individual isotopes of elements); $1\text{u} = 12\text{th}$ of the mass of an atom of a nuclide $^{12}\text{C} \simeq 1.66057 \times 10^{-27}\text{kg}$ — u

French alternative to AU — UA

volt** (electrical potential, potential difference, electromotive force); $1\text{V} = 1\text{W/A} = 1\text{m}^2\cdot\text{kg}\cdot\text{s}^{-3}\cdot\text{A}^{-1}$ — V

watt** (power, radiant flux); $1\text{W} = 1\text{J/s} = 1\text{m}^2\cdot\text{kg}\cdot\text{s}^{-3}$ — W

weber** (magnetic flux); $1\text{WB} = 1\text{V}\cdot\text{s} = 1\text{m}^2\cdot\text{kg}\cdot\text{s}^{-2}\cdot\text{A}^{-1}$ — Wb

watt per square metre** (heat flux density, irradiance) — W/m²

SI PREFIXES
Note: See the introduction for an explanation of the use of prefixes.

exa; $10^{18} = 1\ 000\ 000\ 000\ 000\ 000\ 000$ — E

peta; $10^{15} = 1\ 000\ 000\ 000\ 000\ 000$ — P

tera; $10^{12} = 1\ 000\ 000\ 000\ 000$ — T

giga; $10^9 = 1\ 000\ 000\ 000$ — G

mega; $10^6 = 1\ 000\ 000$ — M

kilo; $10^3 = 1\ 000$ — k

hecto; $10^2 = 100$ — h

deca; $10^1 = 10$ — da

deci; $10^{-1} = 0.1$ — d

centi; $10^{-2} = 0.01$ — c

milli; $10^{-3} = 0.001$ — m

micro; μ
$10^{-6} = 0.000\ 001$

nano;   n
$10^{-9} = 0.000\ 000\ 001$

pico;   p
$10^{-12} = 0.000\ 000\ 000\ 001$

femto;   f
$10^{-15} = 0.000\ 000\ 000\ 000\ 001$

atto;   a
$10^{-18} = 0.000\ 000\ 000\ 000\ 000\ 001$

TRADITIONAL UNITS
including fps units, avoirdupois weight, apothecaries' measures, etc

Note: As with the above international symbols, the symbols in this section normally remain the same whether representing units in the singular or the plural. The units of area or square measure, the square inch, square foot, square yard and so on may be indicated by the symbols in^2, ft^2, and yd^2, etc, or the abbreviations sq in, sq ft, sq yd, etc. Similarly the units of volume or cubic measure, the cubic inch, cubic foot, cubic yard, etc, may be indicated by in^3, ft^3, yd^3 and so on, or cu in, cu ft, cu yd, etc.

alternative to 'ft'   '

alternative to 'in'   "

ounce (apothecaries' weight or   ℥
fluid measure); 1℥ = 8ʒ = 1 Troy
ounce (31.10348g) or 1 fl oz
(28.4131 cm^3)

drachm (apothecaries' weight or   ʒ
fluid measure); 1ʒ = 3Ə
(3.88794 g) or 60♏ (3.55163 cm);
8ʒ = 1℥

scruple (apothecaries' weight);   Ə
1Ə = 20 gr (31.10348 g); 3Ə = 1ʒ

apothecaries' symbol for 'gal'   C

apothecaries' symbol for 'pt'   O

minim (apothecaries' fluid   ♏
measure); 1♏ = 0.059194 cm^3;
60♏ = 1ʒ (fluid)

dry barrel (volume – unit used   bbl
in US); 1 bbl = 7056 in
(115.627 dm^3)

British thermal unit (heat   Btu
energy); 1 Btu (1055.06 J) = the
amount of heat required to raise
1 lb of water at maximum density
through 1 F; 100 000 Btu = 1
therm

bushel (volume); 1 bu (UK) = 8   bu
gal (UK) (36.3687 dm^3); 1 bu (US)
= 64 dry pt (US) (35.2391 dm^3)

hundredweight (mass);   cwt
1 cwt = 4 qr (50.8023 kg);
20 cwt = 1 ton

dry pint (volume – unit used in
dry pt US); 1 dry pt = 0.550610
dm^3; 64 dry pt = 1 bu (US)

degree Fahrenheit (temperature);   °F
the melting point of water is 32°F
and the boiling point of water is
212°F (at 1 standard atmospheric
pressure); temperature degrees
Celsius = 5/9 (temperature degrees
F – 32)

fluid ounce (volume); 1 fl oz   fl oz
(UK) = 1 pt (UK); 1 fl oz
(US) = 29.5735cm^3; 16 fl oz
(US) = 1 liq pt (US)

foot (length); 1 ft = 12 in (0.3048   ft
m exactly); 3ft = 1 yd; 1 US Survey
foot (used by US Coast and
Geodetic Survey) = 1200/3937 m

foot pound force (work energy);   ft lb
1 ft 1 bf = 1·35582 J

foot per second (velocity);   ft/s
1 ft/s = 0.3048 m/s exactly

foot per second squared   ft/s^2
(acceleration);
1 ft/s = 0.3048 m/s^2 exactly

UNITS OF MEASUREMENT

gallon (volume);   gal
1 gal = 4 qt = 8 pt;
1 gal (UK) = 4.54609 dm³;
1 gal (US) = 3.78541 dm³; for 'gal'
as used in geodesy see *International
Units* above

grain (mass); 1 gr = 1/7000 lb   gr
(64.79891 mg exactly);
480 gr = 1 Troy ounce (apothecaries'
ounce)

horse power (power);   hp
1 hp = 745.7 W

inch (length); 1 in = 25.4 mm   in
exactly; 12 in = 1 ft

pound (mass); 1 lb = 16 oz   lb
(0.45359237 kg exactly);
14 lb = 1 st

pound-force (force);   lbf
1 lbf = 4.44822 N

pound-force per square inch   lft/in²
(pressure); 1 lbf/in² = 6894.76 Pa

liquid pint (volume – unit used in   liq pt
US); 1 liq pt = 16 fl oz (US)
(0.473176 dm³); 8 liq pt = 1 gal (US)

mile per hour (velocity); 1 mph   mph
= 1.609344 km/h = 0.44704 m/s
exactly

alternative for mph   mile/h

ounce (mass); 1 oz = 16 drams   oz
(28.3495 g); for Troy ounce see 'ʒ'
above; for fluid ounce see 'fl oz'
above

poundel (force);   pdl
1 pdl = 0.138255 N

pint (volume); 1 pt (UK) = 20 fl oz   pt
(UK) (0.568262 dm³); 2pt = 1 qt;
8pt = 1 gal; see also 'liq pt' and
'dry pt'

quarter (mass); 1 qr = 2 st   qr
(12.7006 kg); 4 qr = 1 cwt

quart (volume); 1 qt = 2pt;   qt
4 qt = 1 gal (see 'gal' above)

stone (mass);   st
1 st = 14 lb (6.35029 kg); 2 st = 1 qr

yard (length); 1 yd = 3 ft   yd
(0.91444 m exactly);
1760 yd = 1 mile

ANSI	American National Standards Institute
BIPM	le Bureau International des Poids et Mesures (the International Bureau of Weights and Measures)
BMR	(Australian) Bureau of Mineral Resources
BS	British Standard
BSI	British Standards Institution
CGPM	la Conférence Générale des Poids et Mesures (the General Conference of Weights and Measures)
CGS	centimetre-gramme-second (system of units of measurement)
CIPM	le Comité International des Poids et Mesures (the International Committee of Weights and Measures)
DIN	Deutsches Institut für Normung (German Institute for Standardization)
ECMT	European Conference of Ministers of Transport
IALA	International Association of Lighthouse Authorities
IEC	International Electrotechnical Commission
IEEE	(American) Institute of Electrical and Electronics Engineers
IHO	International Hydrographic Organisation
IHVE	(British) Institution of Heating and Ventilating Engineers
ISO	International Organisation for Standardization
RIBA	Royal Institute of British Architects
SI	le Système International (d'Unités) (the International System of Units)
UNESCO	United Nations Educational, Scientific and Cultural Organisation
USGS	United States Geological Survey
VDU	visual display unit